THINK AND WIN LIKE VIRAT

SFURTI SAHARE

THINK AND WIN LIKE VIRAT

5 SUCCESS SECRETS

SFURTI SAHARE

JAICO PUBLISHING HOUSE

Ahmedabad Bangalore Chennai
Delhi Hyderabad Kolkata Mumbai

Published by Jaico Publishing House
A-2 Jash Chambers, 7-A Sir Phirozshah Mehta Road
Fort, Mumbai - 400 001
jaicopub@jaicobooks.com
www.jaicobooks.com

THINK AND WIN LIKE VIRAT
ISBN 978-93-48098-57-3

To be sold only in India, Bangladesh, Bhutan,
Pakistan, Nepal, Sri Lanka and the Maldives.

First Jaico Impression: 2025

Page design and layout: Jojy Philip, Delhi

Printed by
Trinity Academy For Corporate Training Limited, Mumbai

CONTENTS

AUTHOR'S NOTE

My journey of writing this book began some time ago. It all started with a proposal I was offered in May 2018, after the launch of my previous national bestseller, *Think and Win like Dhoni*. That was when I began to think about penning a book on another dynamic Indian cricketer Virat Kohli. And yet, I ended up rejecting the offer; you might wonder why. The reason behind it was that I felt I wasn't yet ready to understand Virat or delve into his mind back then.

However, I started to observe him more attentively. It took me a while as I opened up and stretched my mind. Then, I noticed a shift in Virat's character. He began to talk about spirituality, his food habits, and how he changed his mindset. He also focused on how he loved being in a distraction-free environment, and liked to keep things simple for himself. That's when my curiosity piqued. I found his personality intriguing, and wanted to know more about how he thinks and how he does things.

I got going on this book after being inspired by Virat's consistency. That consistency was something I really wanted to have in my life and habits. You see, setbacks tend to reduce my motivation in continuing a habit. In contrast, any such disappointments only seemed to increase Virat's determination, and take him to greater heights. *How does he manage to do that?* I wondered. Every time critics predicted his failure after a dissatisfying performance, he seemed to come back stronger than ever.

As I looked back at Virat's career right from his early days, as I learned details about him through interviews and from previous videos, I found more and more to admire and to emulate in this man. Now, I am a hard-core Virat fan!

Dear reader, if you are completely new to my writing and haven't read my previous books, welcome! This book will guide you in building consistency across everything you pursue, helping you achieve your goals more effectively.

One of my favourite life hacks from the book is summed up as: *"It's boring, deal with it!"* It provides a practical approach to tackling tasks you've been avoiding.

You'll also learn that consistency becomes effortless when your passion drives you to outwork others.

The book is packed with many more insights that can help elevate your performance overall.

It's designed for those who are ambitious, like me, and eager to reach the next level. With Virat's extraordinary discipline and inspiring stories, you can expect your days to become more productive, organized, and focused.

Make it a habit to read this book daily.

Even if you've read it once, I guarantee that every time you open the book again, you'll discover something new and valuable.

If you're one of the numerous people who have read *Think and Win like Dhoni*, thank you, and welcome back! I should tell you, just as MS Dhoni and Virat Kohli are very different individuals, my books about the two of them are quite different too. There's so much to learn from contrasting personalities.

In my debut book on Dhoni, we explored the art of controlling emotions and maintaining balance in both victory and defeat.

The book emphasized the importance of following the process, staying present in the moment, and reading situations effectively. One of its standout lessons was the phrase: "*Try toh karo!*"

We also uncovered six key traits of Dhoni that, when adopted, can transform you into a winner in all aspects of life.

In this book, we'll dive into five key aspects that make Virat the ultimate winner he is today. Through his extraordinary discipline, mindset, and relentless drive, you'll learn how to apply these principles in your own journey toward success.

I hope you gain as much from reading this book as I did from putting it together. Alright then, let's get started on the book without any further ado.

Sfurti signing off, have a great read!

WHY THIS BOOK?

It's 6 p.m. on a Saturday. I'm sitting in my office, all alone. Normally, on Saturdays, we work only until 4 p.m., but I like spending these two extra hours on my own, thinking about how to approach the next week—what to do, what *not* to do, how to take care of various aspects of my life: my business, my writing, my health, my family, and a lot more.

This Saturday, however, something clicked in my head, and a question popped up: "If you had to invest in only one thing today, which asset would it be?" And you know what my answer was? It wasn't gold, properties, stocks, or equities, nor was it about buying an apartment. Instead, the resounding, emphatic answer was... I would invest in my health.

It was right out of the blue—I wasn't sure where this perspective came from.

You see, I have never been obsessed with my health. I love to eat junk food, anything that the tongue craves. I would eat at street stalls, enjoying my *pani puri*, Maggi, or pizza... you name it and I would wolf it down.

Back in 2016, while I was writing *Think and Win like Dhoni* and worrying too much about my career, I developed a condition called acid reflux. After every meal, I would experience a burning sensation near my oesophagus.

Similarly, due to excessive writing while sitting in a closed room, I developed a severe backache caused by two factors: a lack of Vitamin D and poor sitting posture.

I resolved both issues by emulating Virat's fitness regime. In fact, as I sit to write this, I noticed some good sunlight coming into the balcony. Earlier, I would have ignored it, but now I'm disciplined enough to make sure my body gets a healthy dose of sunlight.

All thanks to Virat! When he introduced his fitness regime to the country, it wasn't just for the team—there's a section of people, myself included, who now follow strict fitness routines.

If you're anything like I was before—not caring much about your health—this book will undoubtedly spark a change in you.

I believe my new outlook on the importance of health came about after writing *Think and Win like Virat* at least seven times. Yes, it took me nearly five years to write this book. No kidding. It has been altered and reworked numerous times. Although you're seeing 30,000 words, I think I've written over 3 lakh words. Obviously, after being immersed in intensive writing for this book, I've subconsciously absorbed ideas from its hero, Virat Kohli.

Cracking the Virat Code

The point is not why I have written this book so many times. The point is why wasn't it approved the first few times? And the answer is very simple. The manuscript just was not convincing enough.

Years of observing Virat and trying to put myself in his shoes taught me to work for a vision. Virat has taught me that until I am satisfied, until I am one hundred percent sure that this is my ultimate aspiration, I shouldn't stop. And that's why, despite being rejected several times, I kept on writing, reaching for my vision. I always knew there was going to be something more, a point where the book would just click.

But why Virat? Yes, he is a global cricket superstar and one of India's most celebrated sports icons. But why write a book about him? Why have I spent five years extracting lessons from his life to present to you, my reader? Why not any other cricketer or celebrity? The answer to this is, I saw him change 180 degrees for the better.

He wasn't particularly spiritual, yet he eventually opened himself to receive answers to questions that seem unanswerable.

He has maintained a year-on-year consistency, something that I—and many others—struggle to achieve.

I believe he has learned to tame his restless mind, and the depth he brings to his interviews is something that few celebrities can match. For example, when India won the World Cup, while speaking to the Indian Prime Minister Narendra Modi, Virat said, "*Jab game ko izzat di, game ne wapis izzat di*!" (When you respect the game, the game respects you back!)

This absolute sincerity surprises me. He simply meant, if you give respect to the task, the task will respect you back.

If I give respect to the book, the book will respect me in return. But if I write this book just for the sake of writing, then it will only fulfill its purpose for the sake of appearances.

If you solve math equations just for the sake of solving them or finishing your homework, you'll end up with mediocre results. But if you give your full attention, respect the concept, and dedicate the necessary time, it will reward you with good results.

This is true in business, work, relationships, and everything else.

Ek bar socho toh! (Just think about it once!)

So, all these years, I was waiting for the right spark

to set things in motion, wanting to get into Virat's mindset, to understand how he achieves all that he does. I kept trying to figure out:

- How he thinks
- How he focuses
- How he reacts when things are tough
- How he calms himself down (Yes, he does calm himself, and I will explain this ahead. This is called controlled aggression, which I will discuss in later chapters. Many of us believe he's not calm, but I think we are very wrong to assume that.)
- How he adapts to situations
- How he retains his confidence when things are against him
- How he ensures that no matter how chaotic things get around him, he gives his 100%
- How it's possible for any person to be so consistently excellent

And I do believe I have understood how, although there is still more to the enigma of Virat. Analyzing Virat's strengths has helped me understand how champions become the way they are—how they maintain the highest level of focus, how they make sure that in spite of all the challenging things happening around them, they keep their cool. They make it a point to do justice to their task, no matter what.

In the process of writing this book, I've interviewed many people, watched numerous documentaries, and studied countless innings played by Virat. After all that, I've crafted a well-structured series of five chapters. Following years of gathering insights about Virat, I present to you in this book some of the most inspiring concepts he has taught me.

Virat has always said that he never wanted ordinary things... neither do I. I, too, love the very best of things. But getting to the top-notch level, I have realized, is never going to be easy. After all, my environment and external situation are mostly beyond my control, and often unfavourable—as it would be for many of you, too. So, to get to the best, I will have to control my internal well-being, be it my mental, physical, or emotional health. I'll have to align them in my favour. Maybe that is the reason why it dawned on me that I wanted to invest in my own health—it came from Virat.

Virat has taught me that the human body is a temple; nobody can support you as much as your own body—so take care of it. It was Virat who taught me that if you put your life into everything, then the results will be good. He taught me that whatever you want to do, do it with all your heart, otherwise, don't do it at all.

It was Virat who taught me that no matter what people say, your own convictions should be so strong that outside voices don't matter. From him, I learned about processes, I learned about *junoon* (passion), I learned about how to make sure that you are only pursuing the difficult path. He has taught me that everyone can do what's easy, but if you try to do the difficult things, then automatically you will become exclusive.

He has taught me that scoring runs is not important; scoring runs which will *impact the team and the nation* is important. So, when I work at my office today, I am not just working for the sake of completing a task given by my client. You see, I run Viral Marketing Trends, a digital marketing company. And emulating Virat in my line of work, I make sure that I bring about an impact in the business and the life of my client. When I work with that intention, you know what happens? Everything gets a fresh perspective.

So, over the course of this book I am going to guide you through a lot of ideas that I have mastered while investigating the powerhouse that is Virat Kohli.

Who Is This Book For?

Think and Win like Virat is not just a book; it's a complete guide for people who want to achieve big things—beyond the surface level. If you're aiming to elevate your mind, gain optimal focus, and grow stronger on the inside, no matter how tough things get, then this book is for you.

This book is for those who have already lost much but still believe in that glimmer of hope. It's for those who aren't just dreamers but believers in achieving something meaningful every single day. It's for those who aren't solely focused on results but also care deeply about the process.

Think and Win like Virat is for people who want to create a bigger impact on earth. This book is for those who just don't want to give up. This is for visionaries who know that their dreams are not small... and since their dreams are not small, they will have to work even harder.

So, I am sure this book is for you, my reader, since you were drawn to it. Before you start reading this, however, there are some little things I would like you to keep in mind, and follow:

1. You can read this book multiple times. Carry it with you so that the next time you feel a bit down, take out any page, read any paragraph—I am sure you will feel uplifted and re-energized.
2. As you are reading this book, make sure that you try to keep your own life as the central theme. Don't just be obsessed with Virat Kohli, the sportsman; instead, try to bring out the Virat in you. Take up

your life, take up your situation and just ask yourself the question—what would a legend like Virat do? And the answer to this question would be exactly what you need to do next.

3. Once you finish the full book in sequence, next time you can open it and read from any page. It is going to help you get back your energy, I promise.

Here is a breakdown of the five chapters of this book, so that you can decide where you'd like to start.

Chapter 1: This chapter will help you back yourself. It's only when you support yourself that you can be consistent. This is the master secret I have decoded.

Chapter 2: In the second chapter, I explain the difference between Process-Oriented Goals (POGs) and Result-Oriented Goals (ROGs). Understanding and applying both is crucial for any achievement.

Chapter 3: One of my favourite chapters; this is where I discuss what the *flow* state of mind is. When I write, I don't like to take pauses. Just now, my help offered me coffee which I declined, because I wanted to finish this. I believe I am in a state of flow right now. I will explain more about how to achieve and maintain this state in further sections of the chapter.

Chapter 4: This chapter instructs you on how to make a comeback in life. No matter how successful you become, there are days when you are not at your best—days without clients, days when you fail an exam, or days when relationships falter. This chapter will guide you on how to recover from these setbacks.

Chapter 5: The fifth and final chapter discusses the secret to making it to the next level: *adapting*. It explains how to ensure that you adapt yourself to a level that can propel you far in your life.

So, there you are, all set to enjoy *Think and Win like Virat*. Trust me, you will feel inspired and galvanized as you dip into this book. You see, this is not just a book about cricket; it's a reference guide that has made me super-consistent, super-focused, a super-achiever, and at the same time super-confident—not just about my business, but about my health, my relationships, and everything else in life.

So, read on, and let's start thinking and winning like Virat!

CHAPTER 1

HOW TO ACHIEVE CONSISTENCY

I was struggling to be consistent.

I had the drive, but the massive mood swings were not letting me be consistent.

Some days, I was deeply immersed in my work, and other days, I was just working for the sake of working.

Over the last few years, I have been taking an active interest in Virat's life and routine. Decoding the quick mind of a habitual winner has become my thing.

Then, I read this quote from Virat... he has been saying several times that consistency is boring.

> "Consistency is boring. It's very tough."
>
> — Virat Kohli in an interview with *The Times of India*, July 24, 2019

Virat's statement about consistency being boring opened up a whole new vista for me.

I often hear that consistency is the key to success. "*Be consistent, Sfurti. Wake up on time, maintain a routine,*" they say.

And yet, despite knowing that consistency is key, staying consistent is difficult, isn't it?

The simple acceptance that consistency is boring has helped me drastically in becoming consistent.

Today, I handle my marketing and advertising firm with ease, thanks to my consistency.

I do over 100 events in a year.

I take over 50 flights through the year.

I post a video on Instagram every single day.

I do my yoga routine without fail.

I follow the Vipassana method of meditation.

I write a book every year, and most importantly, I stay away from a lot of shit.

This has only happened since Virat changed my perspective.

And your perspective will change too.

Keep reading, and I bet you will be ten times more consistent and productive than in your previous versions!

I was just a daydreamer before this book happened;

I was only dreaming, and getting frustrated about not achieving those dreams.

Have you ever been like me?

If you have, just keep reading.

I learned something crucial from Virat.

If we can train our minds, and...

If we can convince ourselves that it *has* to be done...

Then we are giving our hopes and dreams a chance to breathe.

So, let's talk about consistency, if you want your dreams take wing.

I believe consistency is easy to achieve when things are in our favour.

Do you agree?

You are scoring good marks, so you are driven to score even better.

You are getting fit and losing stubborn fat, so you are excited to go the gym.

Your boss is praising you, so day by day you are inspired to do well at work.

Your business is growing and there's a constant flow of money, so you are highly motivated to put in more effort in your business.

But the question is...

What if things are not working for you?

What if you go to the gym and don't shed those kilos?

What if your business is failing?

What if you're not scoring enough runs?

What if you are under a lot of pressure?

You know the wonder of Virat? He changed himself completely when he was out of the Indian national cricket team for 11 to 13 months.

When his bat didn't work, he became hyper-focused.

When 50,000 people were booing him, he became hyper-attentive.

When he was at his lowest, he hauled himself to his highest potential.

Read on, and I will teach you how you can become like this. So that you are not just consistent when the winds are in your favour, but you're consistent even when the tide is against you.

How to Be Consistent in Your Lowest Phase

We all know that being consistent is difficult.

But it's even more difficult when you are not getting desired results.

Do you relate?

If you are continuously getting results and excelling, then it's easier to be consistent, as you are excited and motivated to power through all kinds of boredom and mind blocks.

Why?

Because it's the 'excitement' from the previous

victory which will drive you to be consistent. (Miss Excitement is a monkey character from my second book, *The Monkey Theory*. From her, one can learn how the science of excitement works and propels us forward.)

> ***It is easy to find the motivation to work hard and be consistent when one is winning.***

But the vital question is: how to maintain consistency if results are not in your favour?

I am sure all of you have this question in your minds!

I spoke to one of Virat's friends from his childhood—a former IPL cricketer named Rajat Bhatia—in Delhi in June 2024. I did a full podcast with him which is also available on my Instagram.

Virat and Rajat had played together for Delhi.

I was fortunate to have made contact with Rajat and to have a candid conversation with him about Virat and his value system as a sportsman.

Given below are excerpts from our conversation:

Me: "Consistency is something which makes Virat stand out. Over the years, we have seen him go from strength to strength. I understand that it is easy to be consistent when you are performing well, but when results are not in his favour, how does Virat manage it?"

Rajat Bhatia: "Sfurti, I remember this one time when we were in Himachal. We had just returned to our hotel after a domestic match. Virat had performed averagely. While passing by his room, I saw that his door was slightly ajar. I vividly remember that I saw Virat lying on his bed, and staring at the pillow. He looked all tense. His muscles were in knots. I believe he was contemplating about the lost opportunity."

Me, out of curiosity: "What do you think was going on in his mind?"

Rajat: "Well, Virat had just missed an opportunity in the game."

Me: "What do you think he was telling himself?"

Rajat: "He was really backing himself up about the next match. He was telling himself that he can do better than the previous game!"

You know, at that moment, I suddenly drifted into my own thoughts. The last time I didn't close a sales deal, was I backing myself? No. In fact, I was criticizing myself.

I quickly refocused on the interview and asked my next question:

Me: "So, what would Virat tell himself after a loss compared to what other cricketers or performers might say?"

Rajat: "Virat backs himself instead of beating himself up—that's the key difference. Most of us withdraw our own support when things aren't going well."

Me: "Beating themselves up, meaning?"

Rajat: "We usually fill ourselves with self-doubt, get negative, overthink, and question our abilities. But Virat's mindset doesn't allow room for that kind of negativity. He always backs himself."

That was an eye-opener for me too! I sat there questioning my own mindset. How do I react in difficult situations?

Or, if I may ask my readers, what do you do?

I get excited when everything is good—when I am making money and things are golden. But as soon as things stop working in my favour, I lose track and become inconsistent. And from there, the downfall begins.

I would like to share with you, my readers, that if we give space to the feeling of downfall, it holds the potential to spiral right down to the bottom of the pit.

So don't entertain feelings of negativity in times of crisis.

Stand guard to your mind-space, and be consistent, no matter what.

The secret to making 'boring old consistency' interesting is this: back yourself, even after defeat.

Your project hit a setback? Back yourself and finish it anyway—now you have more experience!

Fell off your diet routine? Stop criticizing yourself and get back on track the next day.

Didn't wake up at 5 a.m. today? It's okay. Set the alarm again for tomorrow.

And don't give up.

> "People will always have opinions and judgments, but I have learned to trust my instincts and have confidence in my abilities. This self-belief has been the driving force behind all my achievements on the cricket field."
>
> — Virat Kohli in an interview with *The Times of India*, August 12, 2023

Backing Yourself vs. Beating Yourself

A lot of us do not believe in ourselves and end up lacking motivation, which is one of the major reasons for being inconsistent.

> "I draw inspiration from my past successes and learnings. Reflecting on the moments when I performed at my best and analyzing the areas where I can improve from losses, helps me grow as a player."
>
> — Virat Kohli on August 2023, after knocking off a century against West Indies.

So the question is: how will you back yourself up in situations of crisis, or failure or defeat?

It's very easy to say that if you believe in yourself, you should back yourself! It's easy to say that self-belief is important.

But, imagine the day when everything went against you! Things didn't work out the way they should have, or there was a major setback—you lost a contract or your boss fired you or you lost money.

The crucial question is: *Can you back yourself up at that moment?*

Can you get up the next day and continue your routine?

That's where great people like Virat come into picture. They can really keep up with the boredom of consistency, despite all odds.

How?

By backing themselves up and by not beating themselves up.

I would like my readers to take a moment here. Think of the last crisis that you faced. Think about your state of mind.

Were you angry?

Were you frustrated?

Did you fill yourself up with self-doubt and anxiety?

Did you blame others for the situation?

Did you blame yourself, find faults within, or did you motivate yourself?

Did you take action or did you react?

The answers you give can be an unlearning and relearning process. It will give you a picture of your mental system. You will discover a pattern, and that in turn will help you overcome any negativity that you might have indulged in.

For instance:

- If you are constantly blaming others for your downfall, then you lack ownership of your life.
- If you are blaming yourself, you are just criticizing yourself, you need your support more than anyone.
- If you get frustrated with a setback, then you need to rework on your goal setting (which we will learn in Chapter 2).
- If you are filled with self-doubt, do some great visualization, my friend. (Virat is a fan of visualization by the way.)

On the other hand, if a setback fires you up to get up again and give it another try, to learn from your mistakes, to think progressive as opposed to regressive, and to be in a hopeful space, then you are heading in the right direction.

Lastly, ask yourself, what can I do to back myself when things are not in my favour?

Please do not move on without delving into this question, because it is a very powerful one, and the answer to it has the potential to change your life.

I believe anybody can be consistent when the grass is green, it takes grit when the grass is dry!

Remember Virat's England Tour of 2014? Exactly ten years back from the day I am writing this.

Virat scored 1, 8, 25, 0, 39, 28, 0, 7, 6, and 20 runs in each innings of the five Tests India played, averaging a mere 13.50 per inning.

The world, ranging from social media enthusiasts, fans, and critics, to seasoned journalists, didn't spare him. The roast was real; in fact, media declared that it was the end of Virat Kohli.

It's the same pressure we all face: for not securing an ideal job, for being single, for our physical appearances, for undergoing a divorce, or if your neighbor is doing better than you.

Drawing from my own experience, I know that a slight setback or a minor business loss can spiral me into self-doubt. Questions like '*Am I good enough?*' and '*Should I change my profession?*' flood my mind.

So, nowadays, in any moment of crisis, I ask myself:

What would Virat have done?

The answer is:

He would have reinforced his self-belief.

He would have retained his *consistency.*

He would have backed himself up... every time.

Here are a few instances where you can see Virat in action, backing himself to return stronger than before, each time.

In 2012:

- The media proclaimed that Virat can't play test cricket (this was after his failures in West Indies and England).
- Virat scores a wonderful hundred in an innings against Australia in Adelaide, where the rest of the Indian batsmen failed.

In 2014:

- Media outlets declared that Virat couldn't score runs outside of India in tests (after his poor performance in the England tour).
- Virat scores four centuries in four tests in Australia.

In 2015:

- People said that Virat couldn't lead India in tests.

- Virat leads the Indian team on a 19-match unbeaten streak from 2015 to 2017.

In 2016:

- Some asserted that Virat couldn't score hundreds in T20s, he couldn't score big sixes; he would just rotate the strike.
- Virat scores four centuries in the Indian Premier League, with the most number of sixes in the tournament.

In 2016-17:

- Critics insisted that Virat couldn't score big in test cricket.
- Virat ends up scoring four double hundreds in four series.

In 2018:

- It was alleged that Virat couldn't play the moving ball and so he'd fail in England.
- He becomes the top scorer of the series by scoring 593 runs in 5 matches. Not once was he dismissed by James Anderson.

Of course, some of us might still point out that Virat has never won the IPL. But what I see is that he has won us a great many matches and performed exceptionally. I know few will buy it, but my take on this is: see the half glass full and not the empty bit, dude! We all have our own shares of successes and failures; there are some dreams we aim for, endlessly, without ever reaching. And the journey will still be worth it.

So how do you think Kohli came back stronger each time he was put down by others?

By backing himself, even when others didn't.

If you are wondering about my incessant repetition of this concept of backing oneself up, it's because over the years, I have found that it is one of the most powerful mantras of every successful person. Backing oneself up means:

Rising up with every fall, and being consistent with your routine even if things are not working.

Why?

Because winners understand that nobody can back you the way you can back yourself. It's specific to your mental makeup, and it will only follow *your* orders.

Winners understand that nobody can back you the way you can back yourself.

So, *back yourself* whenever you feel low and defeated and *be consistent*, no matter who says what.

Tell yourself, *"Main kar sakta hun!"* or, *"Main kar sakti hun!"* (I can do it.)

This works.

Ek bar *#trytohkaro*.

Steps to Get Into "Backing Yourself" Mode

I am sure all of you have won many battles in your lives.

- Waking up early in the morning against your wishes is a battle won.
- Studying late nights and early mornings during exam days is a battle won.
- Winning a match against your friend or in a school or college championship is a battle won.
- Choosing healthy food and saying 'no' to your favourite but unhealthy food is a battle won.

In fact, if we look closely and start counting, there are battles to be won each and every day of our lives. But we do it so seamlessly that we are not even aware of it. My suggestion is that when you are feeling down and low, defeated, end-of-the-rope, etc., take a notepad and write down your previous wins.

The wins might be big or small. It doesn't matter.

Let's delve deeper.

It's a real world out there. In a country with a population of 145 crores, you've got to be the best.

> ***If you don't know your game better, you can't excel.***

If you can't excel, you don't find reasons to be consistent. If you are not consistent, you don't get results. If you don't get results, you are not excited. If excitement is not there, passion is totally missing.

Let me put the formula together:

If you know your game better	→	You can excel
If you excel	→	You find reasons to be consistent
If you are consistent	→	You get results
If you get results	→	You are excited
If there's excitement	→	Passion exists

The simple trick I have used is to know my game better, and to be passionate about it.

I get into it totally and work on my strengths, because nobody succeeds by working on their weaknesses.

As you work consistently on your passion, you find yourself discovering new depths of refinement and a kind of mastery that comes only when you attempt something again and again.

Remember, you have to be consistent and dive deep. This is what 99% of the world's population lacks. The remaining 1% is the winner who has all the money, all the success, and all the fame.

In fact, I lacked in achieving this formula for a while too!

- Writing superficially is easy, but connecting each chapter with the next one so that it makes sense to the readers, and helps them weave a path of their own, is difficult.
- Creating content for the sake of creating is easy, but making sure that it will be received well by the readers is hard.
- Appearing for an IIT entrance exam because your parents want you to is easy, but scoring well in it is hard.
- Thinking that I will own a business is easy, but raising funds, doing the marketing, attracting genuine customers, and giving returns to your investors is difficult.

Adhering to the formula above will help you bridge the gap between wishful thinking and achieving your dream.

Stay Away from the Arrogance of the Expert

There is a much-viewed video on YouTube titled 'Virat Kohli: The Complete Batsman | Batting masterclass with Kohli and Nasser Hussain' by *Sky Sports*. In this video, cricket commentator and former cricketer Nasser Hussain interviews Virat, and gets him to demonstrate some of his batting techniques. Check this video out, it's a fun and illuminating watch.

In the video, Hussain notes that Virat has an exceptional speed of hand. At Mohali, none of the Australian bowlers' yorkers seemed to work on him due to his remarkable bat and hand speed. So, he asks Virat whether these high-speed techniques came naturally to him, or whether he had to work on them. Read on to find out Virat's response.

"The bat speed has always been really natural to me but more towards the onside... I've worked on my offside play a lot more. I used to hit past covers a lot and hit straight. But the shot I've developed past point is something that's really helping me now. It's a very minor change and minor adjustment to my grip... and in my stance I just make a small adjustment of opening the bat face a little bit."

See how he acknowledges that he had to work on his offside play. He then goes on to confidently detail several minute technical adjustments he had to learn to make:

1. ***Wider stance:*** He adopted a slightly wider stance, allowing him greater balance and stability at the crease. This change gave him a better base to play the swinging ball, making him less prone to edging to the slip cordon.
2. ***Playing late:*** He worked on playing the ball much later, especially in conditions where the ball swings considerably. By playing the ball closer to his body,

he reduced the chances of edges carrying to the slip cordon.

3. ***Adjusting the bat path:*** He refined the path of his bat swing, ensuring it was coming down straighter and more in line with the ball. This adjustment minimized the bat's angle at the point of contact, reducing the risk of edges.
4. ***Mental adjustment:*** Beyond the technical, Virat Virat's biggest transformation was perhaps mental. He demonstrated immense discipline, choosing to leave balls outside the off-stump that he might have previously chased. This restraint allowed him to better manage the swinging deliveries, choosing to score off balls that were safely within his reach.

Batting is his core strength—Virat is a batsman. So, he identified the specifics of the little loopholes in his play, and plugged them to make his strength even more potent.

You might think this is as easy as it sounds, but it is not.

Let's think about this. Virat is a world-class batsman; his name is taken alongside legends of the cricketing world. His name will one day likely find place in the ICC Hall of Fame, and he is well aware of it. Despite all this, he admitted to himself and to the world that his offside needs work, and so, he went and worked on it. He emerged stronger and better.

Have you heard of the phenomenon named 'the arrogance of the intellect'? Sometimes, intellectuals look down on conversing with average people, since their thoughts are too difficult for most people to understand. Similarly, when a person is good at something—whether it's batting in cricket or at conducting research in physics—they become so arrogant that they refuse to admit the little mistakes they make. However, both the batsman and the researcher need to acknowledge loopholes in their 'game' to plug them, to become exceptional.

Some examples:

1. A born artist refuses to go to art school to better their craft because they feel that they know it all. They do not accept that their skills can be polished further at art school.
2. People who started working before the digital revolution typically refuse to learn the basics of computers because they are now professionals. Learning something new hurts their ego.
3. People in the IT field refuse to learn rudimentary commerce because they believe that their skill is superior to that of the commercial field. But in today's professional world, a little knowledge of both commerce and IT is absolutely essential, and it supports your existing skills.

In the interview earlier, Virat displays supreme confidence in his abilities as a batsman while also admitting his shortcomings. His answer is an adept demonstration in *avoiding arrogance* and working on weaknesses by *diving into the depths* of his game, to achieve excellence. We, too, need to keep our minds open to our imperfections, so that we can fix them. The arrogance of the expert can be a huge deterrent.

And please note—the arrogance of not accepting flaws can make you inconsistent. These are contradictory values. If consistency is the key to success, arrogance is the key to failure.

And while I am saying all these, I would like to reiterate that the whole process of fixing these weaknesses might be boring. But it will have to be done if one wants to excel in one's chosen path.

In fact, I remember falling into the trap of arrogance myself!

After writing two books and delivering major TEDx talks, I thought I was an excellent public speaker and didn't need any fine-tuning.

For the longest time, I believed I was naturally talented, and that over-preparation might ruin my performance. I wasn't ready to acknowledge my flaws. Even when people pointed out technical errors, I defended them as 'my style'.

But when my growth started to plateau—perhaps

because I refused to accept my shortcomings—I realized the mistake I had made.

I've seen many professionals, cricketers, and artists fall into this same trap after early success.

Think about it.

Have you ever felt that you are too good to change?

I am sure there must have been an incident you remember where you felt this way.

If yes, let's accept and start fine-tuning our craft because it's the only way we grow.

The Magic Ingredient

So far, we have discussed about how to:

- Back yourself even when things are not so good
- Accept the fact that consistency is boring and still go along
- Up your game by diving into it fully

We have talked about consistency, the factors that can affect it, and what needs to be done to overcome those obstacles to stay consistent and excel.

Now, we're going to be discussing something that is closest to my heart. As I'm writing this, my fingers are tickling with excitement, and I am feeling overwhelmed.

I am pumped to talk about... *Junoon!*

Yes, it compensates for the boredom along the way...

It makes up for the losses and keeps despair at bay!

It's the *junoon,* the passion, which makes Virat so special!

The closest word in English for *junoon* is passion. But I am going to use '*junoon*' in this book because I believe it packs more power. I request you, my dear reader, to energize the word as if it's a divine power, and to use it regularly in your vocabulary.

It was 5:25 in the morning when I was waiting for my flight to Delhi at the Pune Airport. Kapil Dev, one of my favourite all-rounders, happened to be along with me on the same flight.

So, early that morning, I gave him my book and he said, "Oh, *you* have written this book! I saw it somewhere."

I told him that right now I was working on a book on Virat, and wanted to know his views on Virat.

I asked him, "What makes Virat so special? What does he have that makes him exceptional, and how does he manage to stay that way, so consistently?"

Instead of answering me right away, he responded to my question with a volley of counter-questions. "How did you manage to write such an insightful book at your age? How did you manage to sell so many copies of the book? You train people, and you travel across the world all on your own. You handle your business, both of your books are popular... How did you do that? Who gave you this idea of so many monkeys and their interpretations? This is no small work; how do you manage to do all this?" And so on.

I almost instantly answered, "I just love it!"

And Kapil said, "*Wo junoon hai aap se har cheez karata hai!*" (It is that *passion* you have that makes you do it all.)

He continued, "You want to know what makes Virat, 'The Virat'? The answer lies within you—*junoon.* If you want to catch the magic of Virat, catch his *junoon. Junoon* should be enough to ferry you through all rough waters." He smiled. "When you are passionate about something, you are in that state of equilibrium with your mind, body, and space. It's just that work that you care about, and that's the key!" he added.

We will speak about *junoon* now. Let's first listen to a story.

In the 2016 IPL, Virat played with nine stitches on his hand. If you type 'Kohli stitches' into Google, you'll see them for yourself. I encourage my readers to look it up and witness his *junoon* for cricket.

After getting those nine stitches, most people would have taken time off. I might have pampered myself endlessly. But here comes King Kohli and scores a century in the very next match!

What kind of passion and madness is this?

He scored 113 off 50 balls against KXIP with nine stitches in his hand, in a 15-over game.

When Virat was young, he thrived on challenges. He used to say to his coach, Rajkumar Sharma, '*Yeh chote wale toh mujhe out hi nahi karte... Mujhe U-15 group mein khelna hai.*' (These younger boys never dismiss me... I want to play in the Under-15 group.)

This is what *junoon* does to you. You don't fear challenges—you're driven to conquer them. All you want is to taste greatness.

Your *Junoon* Is Your Therapy

Are you passionate about your work?

A couple of years ago I was invited to a TED talk in Italy. They wanted me to speak on a topic that changed my life, and could have a positive effect on the listeners.

The topic I chose was *junoon*. I wove my speech around the idea of passion, and how, if a person gets intoxicated on passion, they do not need anything else to give them their life's high. They will never need to smoke, use substances, or even drink a glass of wine to feel great. Their *junoon*. on its own is elevating. I named the talk '*I Don't Need a Glass of Wine to Get My High!*'

I was pretty young then, but my talk received a standing ovation. I stood there in the middle of the stage, savouring the moment. I understood that my words connected with those people, and that's why they were so moved by them. They resonated with the idea that *junoon* is the only trait that can activate the winner within us.

I think that when you surrender to your *junoon*, you don't need anything else.

Your work becomes a therapy.

> "A good cover drive is therapeutic."
>
> — Virat Kohli tweeted on November 1, 2019

This is what Virat tweeted after playing a Test series against South Africa.

Each week, I see people seeking medical help and therapy to be happy. Carl Vendette, a corporate senior manager in Canada, went public about his battle with depression. In one of his talks, he said something super meaningful, "A job you feel good about is therapeutic."

For how many people is their work therapeutic?

Very few, right? Most people dislike their jobs.

Unless their job is *junoon*-driven.

Without *junoon*, your goals are directionless.

> ***Without goals, becoming a genius remains just a dream.***

So, let me make things simple for people who find it difficult to work hard, make a career, or be successful. You need to find your *junoon*.

These days, I see a new trend among youngsters. They sit at home doing nothing, because there are so many options, and they don't know what to do.

This is not an arbitrary statement.

I have two clients, both in the age bracket of 21 to 28, who cannot commit themselves to a job. They believe that if they commit to one career, they will miss out on so many other options that are available. Once or twice, they did get a job, but quit in three months' time because they got 'bored'.

So, I am working with them to facilitate them on a quest to find their *junoon*. Once they hit that jackpot, the rest will be a cakewalk.

The purpose of this book is not to just give you a read about Virat, one of the most formidable batsmen in the cricket today, but to make you a Virat of your industry.

Further, I am going to give you certain examples which will help you identify how and why you are unable to amplify your *junoon*.

Why Is '*Junoon*' Worth Living For?

Whatever Virat is today, I believe he is the product of his absolute *junoon*.

That *junoon* which makes you single-minded, which helps you prioritize things...

Which helps you be in that zone where there is no room for any doubt.

I have learned a Japanese concept called *zanshin*, which is '*aiming without aiming*'.

I am going to speak about it in a later part of the book, but the core idea of *zanshin* is to enter a state of performance, where you become limitless.

Many athletes call it entering into their *zone*. Only your *junoon* can help you get to that zone.

Now let's study a little more about Virat.

In 2008, Virat got us the World Cup U-19 as captain. He was barely 18 years old then. Later, he was picked up by Royal Challengers Bangalore.

Let me show you the statistics of his entire IPL performance. Pay special attention to the first six years.

- Runs scored in 2008 - 165 runs
- Runs scored in 2009 - 246 runs
- Runs scored in 2010 - 307 runs
- Runs scored in 2011 - 557 runs
- Runs scored in 2012 - 364 runs
- Runs scored in 2013 - 634 runs
- Runs scored in 2014 - 359 runs
- Runs scored in 2015 - 505 runs
- Runs scored in 2016 - 973 runs

- Runs scored in 2017 - 308 runs
- Runs scored in 2018 - 530 runs
- Runs scored in 2019 - 464 runs
- Runs scored in 2020 - 466 runs
- Runs scored in 2021 - 405 runs
- Runs scored in 2022 - 341 runs
- Runs scored in 2023 - 639 runs
- Runs scored in 2024 - 741 runs

As you must have noticed, Virat's batting numbers are not a straight line upwards. There are some years with high stats followed by low ones. Now imagine the pressure on him after one bad tournament.

To an average person, handling a setback is one of the most difficult things.

Now, here comes Virat, playing his first IPL with an average of 15 runs per match. Can you imagine the pressure he must have been under?

It's crazy.

So, who or what came to the rescue?

It's his *junoon!*

The *junoon* to play for India, and to become one of the best in the world.

If you are struggling with a bad patch, it's also because your skills do not match the results you are expecting. Maybe your *junoon* has faded.

Recharge it, buddy!

Feel excited about living it.

Look at what Virat achieved in the IPL.

In the 2016 IPL, Virat's 973 runs got him an Orange Cap.

In 2018, RCB retained him for ₹17 crores.

In 2019, he became the second player in the IPL to score 5,000 runs.

Your *junoon* can help you handle all the tough waves.

If you have it, just preserve it; if you don't have it, just find it.

In the Australian Cricket Web Series called 'The Test' on Amazon Prime (Season 1, Episodes 3 and 4), I saw how the Aussies were getting mad at Virat.

> "He (Virat) wants to show 'I'm here to dominate Australia', that's his mindset coming out."
>
> — Brad Haddin, Australian Fielding Coach

> "I want him (Virat) completely ignored. I don't want anyone engaging with him. We just flat out ignore him."
>
> — Tim Paine, Former Australian Cricketer

> *"India outplayed us. They were hungry. I've never seen an Indian team fight like that before."*
>
> — Nathan Lyon, Australian Bowler

They were visibly frustrated and annoyed because of his temperament, so much so that it was a hot topic of discussion.

In the end, Virat's commitment and determination made India win in Australia.

I suggest you watch that particular match, or at least the highlights. This win made me so proud of being an Indian.

Especially, when an Indian was troubling all the 11 Aussies were sitting and brainstorming on how to take his wicket in the dressing room.

This level of impact is not possible without a thick share of boring days.

What I mean to say is: follow the *junoon*, but be ready to digest the boredom of consistency.

Accept that it's going to be there.

In fact, welcome it with an understanding that if you are not going crazy with boredom because of the time you are investing, because of the repetitive nature of the work, 16 hours of studies (for example), doing the same thing over and over, with or without any result, then, my friend, you are probably not doing enough. Find excitement in that very boredom. Put a poster on the wall that says: 'Virat gets bored with his routine and that makes him a winner. When I too get bored with my hard work, I too will become a winner!'

This will keep you from giving up.

Also, learn to back yourself in crises.

As Virat says, *"I have to believe that I am the best!"* (He said this during an interaction with Dinesh Karthik, cricket expert and commentator for *Sky Sports*.)

And now, all you people who are trying to find their *junoon*, here are some simple tips for you!

How to Ignite That *Junoon*?

1. Associate yourself with a bigger purpose

> *Associate your goal with a purpose that can serve as a greater good for the people around you.*

For example:

I try to do my best at my work because I have employees in my office, and they work to support their families. If I don't give it my best and my work fails, then my employees will be directly affected. Also, I like to believe that my coaching, training, and my books add value to the lives of people. So, my work is not just about me, it affects or touches a few more lives.

Virat's life is surrounded by a huge array of people. He has his team of managers, physical trainers, dietitians, mental health coaches, and a miscellany of others. If he does not give his best and fails, this entire support system of his that survives because of him, will collapse, too.

In my case, it is about the 50 people who work for me and the numerous readers who value my books. For Virat, it's about the '*aan, baan, shaan*' (dignity and honour) of the whole nation.

His purpose is bigger, so his *junoon* has to be big, his consistency has to be world class, and his success equally huge.

You want to make it as big as Virat?

Paint a big picture of your *junoon*, and chase it with consistency.

Be bored, but chase it.

> ***Your junoon should drive you to consistency.***

So the crux of what I'm saying is, when you feel down, your purpose will come to your rescue!

Virat tells us several times that the *junoon* to play for the country drives him to score those big hundreds!

If your *purpose* is strong and you consistently back it up, *results* will appear.

I was interviewing Ekta Bisht, one of the players in the Indian Women's Cricket Team. The *junoon* and the pride to play for the country, and produce a win was quite evident.

When you do anything with that *junoon*, new doors open; that vision can make you absolutely bulletproof against all odds.

In the next chapter, I am going to speak about how to set goals and go about them.

The concept of process-oriented goals and result-oriented goals helped me strike the right balance in the kind of work I do. Maybe it will help you too.

The Bottom Line

- Consistency in practice is the key to excellence.
- You're not doing things right if you're not bored out of your mind. The path towards excellence might be boring, but the results will be worth it.
- Logic can take you from A to B, but the magic of *junoon* can take you from A to infinity.
- Passion has power; follow it.
- Support yourself in times of crisis, rather than being self-critical.
- Write down what you want to achieve and be passionate about it. This will help you grow and also prevent discouragement.
- Don't read this book at night and then sleep on it. Read it in the morning; *dream while awake, and take action.*

CHAPTER 2

THE ART OF GOAL SETTING

I am personally curious as to what kind of preparation goes into building the biggest brands of the country.

I am sure it's not just me. A lot of Gen Z and Millennials are working hard to become the most eligible person for the country.

But this journey will need some discipline, as we have learned from Virat. We cannot become dead-afraid zombies executing tasks; we need to be playful, confident, and masters of execution.

This chapter opens a whole new horizon to goal-setting, balance, and pushing yourself inch by inch. But first we're going to look at a pivotal component required to do all this. Read on!

> "I visualize tough situations and then find solutions… The ability to think otherwise in a difficult situation is something that sets you apart in that situation…"
>
> — Virat Kohli, *The Times of India*, June 18, 2017

Visualization

I learned a very important thing from Virat; the first thing we should be doing before trying to achieve anything is *visualization.*

You know guys, I, as an individual, pray for easy solutions. I always blame circumstances if situations turn against me.

I am constantly like, "Why me?"

But Virat believes in saying, "Try me!"

Guys, we have to admit, cricket is one of the most competitive of sports. The highest levels of preparations are needed.

And distractions are many around us.

All we need is the right process, so one of the top things we have to learn from Virat is visualization.

Virat has been seen reading *The Secret* by Rhonda Byrne. It's one of my favourite books, and I have been very vocal about it from a long time. But there's a difference between reading it and applying it a few times, versus reading it and applying it consistently. Visualization is a powerful tool described in this book.

> "I visualize a lot, and I see myself in difficult situations and actually convince myself that I can pull the team out in those situations. It won't happen every time, but every 8 out of 10 times, it will end up happening, because you are so convinced about it."
>
> — Virat Kohli, *The Times of India*, June 18, 2017

Average people like us may know the formula, but we rarely use it. People like Virat, however, are disciplined enough to put it into practice.

> ***The first step to setting goals and achieving them would be*** **visualization.**

I shall explain this in detail in the later chapters.

Let's look at a few instances when Virat's visualization helped him.

Virat spoke about visualization during his 'In Depth with Graham Bensinger' interview in August 2021. "It (visualization) is everything for me... I literally sat down 2-3 months before (an overseas tour) and I've made a decision in my head that I'm going to take their best bowler on. And when I train in the gym, when I'm practicing, regularly there are visuals running in my head (of) me dominating that bowler... I'm putting myself in a situation where that guy's bringing the heat onto me and I'm countering that, and you know that becomes such a reality in your head and invariably when I went into that situation I ended up dominating that guy in their own home conditions"

Virat is very clear about how, months before every match, he visualizes the toughest situation he could possibly encounter, and he imagines himself "dominating" every challenge.

What do we do in such situations?

Personally, I wouldn't even imagine such scenarios—I console myself by thinking, 'Why borrow trouble?' I've noticed many people do the same, with a mindset of 'We'll deal with it when it happens.' We all pray for things to go well, but we never think about how we can actually overcome challenges.

But does this approach prepare us mentally? What if we imagined our biggest challenges and visualized ourselves overcoming them?

In June 17, 2017, *The Times of India* carried an article on Virat with the headline 'I visualize tough situations and find solutions: Virat Kolhi'. When Virat was asked about how he prepares for big game, he said, "If you are thinking we are three down but I am going to counterattack and get the team back on track, *it ends up happening because you are convinced about it.*"

Virat has complete faith in himself that even if his team is three wickets down, he will still back his team and they will win.

In my world, that would be like believing I can bounce back from bankruptcy. Jokes aside, what if you imagine yourself setting up a business, and nothing went according to plan but you visualize yourself dominating everything.

What if, while preparing for IIT-JEE, you visualize yourself getting the highest score.

What if you imagine getting fired from your current job, and visualize acing the interview for that dream job you always wanted.

Dare to visualize the toughest situations, with you rising like a phoenix to come back stronger.

This can be a pivotal step in goal setting—first, visualize the outcome.

In February 2023, *ANI* carried an article that talks about how Virat used visualization to better his test score. Virat spoke about the vitriol that was hurled at him after India lost the first two matches of a series in Australia. The entire Indian team was tense, and he was the newest member. He said, "How am I going to turn this around? I told myself, 'Hold on, maybe I can be different if I think differently.' I kept telling myself I am good enough and I can do it. I ended up scoring 48 in the first innings and 75 in the second in that Test match. That made me believe that the power of visualization and belief in yourself is so huge, we never fully tap into the potential like that..."

Let all of us try to learn from what Virat achieved here. He was under immense pressure, kept getting thoughts of self-doubt, and even his team started believing they would lose. He stopped, processed his thoughts, and realized he was going about everything completely wrong. He instantly changed his thinking. He literally manifested his win into reality.

I want you, readers, to take this learning and apply it to your own lives. Your life could reach its lowest point; instead of drowning in self-pity and reassuring yourself saying '*koi nahi, life hai*' (It's okay, it's just life), just try backing yourself and visualizing winning. Visualize it vividly. Strongly. Put all your energy into believing that you are good enough, you can definitely do it. Virat spoke about the immense potential of visualization, let us also try it ourselves.

That would be the first step in goal setting.

A Zen State of Mind

My good friend Ravish Bisht, a top broadcast journalist and sports anchor, told me this story about Virat while we chatted in December 2023.

Bisht was in Sydney covering the India vs. Australia tournament. Virat and the entire team was about to arrive for a match.

He said there were many Virat fans waiting for him. So many that Virat signed autographs and clicked selfies for almost 25 minutes.

Then he said this to the fans, "*Ab hogaya, ab mujhe practice karne do*!" ("It's enough now. Please let me practice.")

He then went on to practice and was in ultra-focused mode for at least two and a half hours!

Doesn't it give us perspective that when you are doing something, focus on it 100%? Virat wouldn't dilute any task.

Ravish further added, "Sfurti, you know, when I sit in press conferences and take his interview, I sometimes feel like Arjuna is sitting beside me. He gives you full focus and amazing intensity! With steady eyes, he smiles with calm as if in a zen state. Have you noticed his smile?" he asked me. "You should observe it. It's a beautiful smile and reflects his strength of character."

Ravish spoke further about Virat's smile and his calm, zen-like demeanor. As I listened, I found myself wanting to achieve that state of being—I wanted to achieve zen.

Virat himself has mentioned in several interviews that when he steps onto the field, he doesn't notice the 50,000 people booing him. He focuses only on the ball and sees it as an opportunity.

I want my readers to achieve zen as well!

So, what does it mean to be 'zen'? According to the Merriam-Webster Dictionary, being zen is:

'A state of calm attentiveness in which one's actions are guided by intuition rather than by conscious effort.'

Please keep in mind that this is different from 'Zen' (with a capital Z), which refers to a sect of Buddhism. Being 'zen,' in this context, means being completely present in a calm, focused way, where actions flow naturally without effort.

Spending 25 minutes clicking selfies with fans and signing autographs is a long time, but Virat did it because (a) he wanted to, and (b) as a celebrity, it's part of what's expected.

Giving his fans 100% is an example of being in a zen state of mind.

Focusing 100% during cricket practice also requires a zen state of mind.

Getting a good night's sleep without obsessing over every little thing he could've done differently demands a zen state of mind.

And maintaining a strict diet to stay fit and perform at his best—this, too, calls for a zen state of mind.

> ***We all have 24 hours in a day, during which we do what we believe is our best. But did we really give it our all?***

Virat's zen-like mindset is what enables him to focus intensely on the present and keep pushing his limits. He achieves, while the rest of us often struggle.

If you have big goals, many elements need to come together perfectly for you to achieve them successfully.

For Virat, in order to become the best:

1) He has to practice everyday
2) He has to workout daily
3) He has to eat according to a strict routine
4) He has to rest
5) He has to relax
6) He has to be mentally agile
7) He has to spend time with family
8) He has to groom himself to be media ready
9) He has to make the press happy
10) He has to keep his fans happy
11) He has to spend time with his friends
12) He has to do endorsements

And on and on... I have listed some 12 points off the top of my head; you can add several more, I'm sure. You get my drift. Everything *has* to be done. And to be able to do all this, one needs to be very zen. Diluting tasks or responsibilities or attention or focus will mean a downfall into oblivion.

As I am writing this chapter, I know I can't reduce my focus and run to a meeting. Months and months of research is now taking shape. I have to keep my mind calm and steady so that I can focus and deliver.

For me, this is what happens:

One half of my work is very dynamic. I have to meet clients and stakeholders. I have to discuss plans and strategies. I have to see through executions, fly to meet prospective clients, and be a functional family person as well.

The other half of my work needs me to be more stable, cool, and calm. My mind needs to be quiet and steady, because this involves research for writing my current book.

I had the tendency to think about my book when I was running around during the day, and to think about the next day's work and clients as I was sitting with my book, writing.

Nothing worked.

And then, during my research for this book, I learned about this zen state of being that is absolutely necessary if one wants to achieve their goals. When you are in a zen state, you are ultra-focused. In this condition, work doesn't need to be done. Work just happens.

I block my time like Virat. I got this idea from Ravish when he explained how Virat signed autographs and then immediately shifted focus to practice.

When I go to the office, I divide my time into blocks. I promise myself that I'll work distraction-free for the next 50 minutes—turning off my phone, ignoring notifications, and creating a focused zone to get 100% involved in the task.

The level of focus I achieve afterward is tremendous.

The human brain produces its best output under such intense focus.

This is what Virat has—he maintains his ultra-focus through a zen state of being. And this is the second step we should take on our own quest towards our goals.

Virat's Process of Continuous Improvement

When I think about Virat and his journey, I see a reflection of my own path in a different field.

Just as Virat set his sights on playing for India from a young age, I too had my dreams. They may not have been on the cricket field, but the essence of dedication and focus was the same.

Virat's process of believing in himself and getting the 'boring' tasks done deeply resonates with me. In his youth, he set a clear goal to play for India. His dedication to cricket from a very young age demonstrates his unwavering commitment. Recognizing the growing importance of fitness in modern cricket, Virat underwent a major transformation—setting strict fitness goals, changing his diet and training regimen. This not only improved his game, but also set a new standard for the team.

Every step Virat took, from focusing on fitness to adapting his style for different formats, reminds me of how I approached my career.

So, my friend, please try and look for similarities between your endeavors and Virat's path, too. This will help you take away lessons from his approach and apply them in yours.

Initially, Virat had a tendency to play rash shots. He then set a goal to refine his technique, especially in handling swing bowling outside the off-stump. This was evident during India's tour of England in 2018, where he emerged as the top scorer, showcasing his improved technique against the swinging ball.

I became curious—how does Virat keep turning up as an improved version of himself?

Here is the answer I have deduced, and it outlines Virat's process:

Observe + Analyze → Simplify in your head →
Create balanced goals → Back yourself

These are the steps Virat takes when setting his goals:

Step 1: Observe and analyze

Step 2: Simplify the goal

Step 3: Create balanced goals

Step 4: Back yourself

Let's look at each of these steps in detail. I won't go into Step 4—backing yourself—since we've already spoken about that extensively in Chapter 1.

1. Observe and analyze

I recall the example I gave in the beginning of Chapter 1—when Virat was lying on his bed after a bad match. That was a classic example of him analyzing.

> "The most difficult thing in cricket is not about opponents and what you know about them, it's what you know about yourself and your strengths."
>
> — Rajat Bhatia, Former KKR Player in the Indian Premier League

Rajat explained that he had seen many cricketers in his life. After all, he had been playing in the domestic circuits, and in the IPLs. So, he knew that most cricketers would analyze their opponents, which *is* an important thing.

But more than that, Rajat believes that the most essential thing is to go deep inside oneself to analyze our strengths, our weaknesses, what needs to be honed, and what should be eliminated.

"Virat clearly knew that if he wants to be in the game, he will have to become disciplined," said Rajat.

He explained how, in pursuit of perfection, he (Virat) later ended up changing his diet and his sleeping habits.

Rajat said, "Virat used to mimic me. He is very good at mimicry. He used to mimic how I used to give instructions, and in fact, even the way I was walking. That's good observation skill."

"I have seen that he (Virat) understood that confidence is a must in cricket! So, no matter how many times a bowler has troubled Virat, he would always believe that he can outperform him."

Rajat continued "For instance, Amit Mishra often troubled Virat with his bowling. But whenever Virat was batting next, his body language would always dominate the bowler, thus not allowing the bowler to perform at his peak."

Observation is key.

So, as you're reading this, the first thing you will have to do for your goals is to observe yourself as well as others, and then analyze what needs to be done.

Virat's method of 'observe and analyze' is fundamental in any field.

For a startup, this means constantly analyzing market trends, consumer behaviour and competitors' strategies.

Virat's approach to refining his cricket batting

technique, through observation, mirrors a valuable strategy for startup owners and individuals who want to plug their shortcomings and achieve success.

His ability to recognize a specific area of weakness—handling swing bowling—and diligently working to improve it, is a lesson in targeted skill development.

For a startup owner, this translates to identifying key areas in their business that require improvement—be it marketing, product development, or customer service, and then dedicating resources and time to enhancing these areas.

Observation leads to insights that can pivot a startup towards success. In a large firm, a CEO must observe both the internal dynamics of the company, and the external business environment. This helps in making informed decisions that are aligned with both the company's goals and market demands.

Adaptability is another lesson from Virat's journey. His ability to adapt his playing style to different conditions and formats is a classic application of excellent observation. Startups often operate in a dynamic environment, and being adaptable can mean the difference between thriving and failing.

Australian spinner Brad Hogg was quoted by *Hindustan Times* in an article in 2022: "When you have got the talent, you know what to do and it is all about the attitude and the mindset when you go out there on the day. So I think it is more just the preparation before the game and not so much out in the middle. We know he has got skills and he can take on any bowler in the world. Is he getting the right resources and time management to make sure he is mentally relaxed before the game?"

Virat knew exactly when to practice, and when to mentally relax.

This balance is important to understand. Sometimes the mind needs to be composed and relaxed, whereas sometimes that aggression is important.

The situational reading of the game or of the market is a crucial skill.

Take the following story, for instance.

It's the second ODI in an India vs. Australia series, on January 17, 2020. I am in front of my TV while writing this. India had lost their first match in the three-match series in Mumbai, by 10 wickets. This was India's biggest loss in many, many years.

Now, India was batting first, and to survive in the game, it was important for India to score 320+ runs. After Rohit Sharma got dismissed, Virat came up to bat.

I have recorded a LinkedIn video on how Virat rises up to this occasion, but this time I want to go into the depth of it.

Virat was scoring only singles. That's it! Even with the loose deliveries coming in, he kept defending. Virat scored around 78 runs, but his first 50 came in 50 balls.

Although the Australians were trying to tempt him, Virat kept at his defense. He proved to everybody the truth of the adage 'the best defense is a good offense'.

Virat knows that not every battle is meant to be won, not every ball is a six. When he hits a six, his next ball is always a single run. Why? Because he knows that the bowler is now alert and will anticipate his six. He understands that defense is as important as attack.

Knowing when to attack, and when to defend, is a game of observation.

In the corporate world, this boils down to understanding market trends and competitors before launching new products or strategies. Rushing in without careful observation can lead to significant losses. Startups, especially, need this approach. With limited resources, they can't afford to attack recklessly. They must observe, learn, and then strike.

In relationships, too, sometimes just listening and understanding before responding can prevent conflicts and strengthen bonds. Quick judgments or reactions without observation often lead to misunderstandings.

For our mental health and our daily routines, observing our own habits, thoughts, and behaviohrs is essential. It helps us identify patterns that might be detrimental. This self-awareness allows us to make necessary adjustments, leading to a healthier, more balanced life.

2. Simplify the goal for your mind

I was sitting in my hostel room in 2012, completely absorbed in the 11th match of the Commonwealth Bank Series at Hobart, where India was up against Sri Lanka. I remember it was February 28, barely a month ahead of my birthday on March 22.

Facing Sri Lanka, a tough team of that time, India had a challenging task ahead. They were chasing 321 runs in a 50 over game back in 2012, when anything above 300 was a real task. It felt like India had a mountain to climb.

The game kicked off with Sachin Tendulkar and Virender Sehwag giving us a hopeful start, but they got dismissed early; India was on the verge of a loss. Then came Gautam Gambhir but he, too, was run out. It was then Virat and Suresh Raina stepped into the spotlight.

We won that game by the 36th over. And Virat scored 133 runs.

Much later, in an Instagram live, when asked a question about this spectacular win, Virat revealed that he and Suresh Raina had strategized the breakdown of the target as if they were playing two T20 matches. "He (Suresh Raina) and I discussed that we need to break it down into two T20 games and that was the first kind of revelation for chasing the big totals for me."

He just made the target simple for his mind.

See, what normally happens is, if you see 321 runs required to be scored, it seems too big a task. If you see it as two T20s in a row however, then it's quite simple.

Such a straightforward yet ingenious approach! It was like transforming a daunting task into an achievable, almost playful, challenge.

Virat scored 133 runs in 86 balls, with Suresh Raina providing stellar support. The mood in my hostel room transformed from tense to excited. The duo wasn't just playing; they were demonstrating how to dissect a challenge into smaller, more manageable parts.

Scoring 200 runs in a T20 match is easy, and many teams have attained it. In simple terms, Virat suggested to Suresh Raina—let's play the first 20 overs as if we are playing one T20 match and then play another T20 match from the 21st to 40th over. If we have a shortfall, we will still have last 10 overs to make it up. India ended up reaching the target by the 36th over.

That match, especially Virat's method, turned into a personal life lesson for me.

> ***Complex goals make it very difficult to act on them.***

Remember, the idea behind setting goals is not to set goals, but *to act* on them. Unless our brain has clarity about our goals, it will not make it easy for us to work on them.

Giving a personal example to illustrate the point—writing a book is a vague goal. To make it easy, I can decide to write one chapter a week. I know it's simple for me, and as I have only five chapters in my book, I can make it happen in just five weeks. If I set the goal this way, my mind knows that I will need not more than one hour a day, and that sounds a pretty workable plan. Now, I know that I can make time for other priorities and still finish my book. I know I can take out some time to play or to do something which I love, and even have fun, while still aiming for my goal.

This is true for how Dhoni worked as well. The following is the example I had mentioned in my book *Think and Win like Dhoni*.

How does Dhoni strategize 200 runs in a T20 game? The answer is a simple equation. The team calculates that they have to hit 20 fours and their six batsmen can do it, so the math is:

20 balls X 4 runs = 80 runs are made in 20 balls.

Now, in 100 balls the team will need 120 runs, which is quite an easy target for the mind. This simplification helps the team stay calm and execute their plan of action, rather than being stressed by a seemingly difficult target.

As a Virat fan, I want to strongly give you the message:

Free yourself from people's opinions and their expectations.

Keep it simple.

For Kohli, it's a bat and ball.

For me, it's a book and pen.

For you, it's target and execution.

Nothing else in between.

It's the goal minus everything else.

3. Create balanced goals

MS Dhoni always kept saying this, and now Virat does, too! They both say: *Process is more important than the results.*

If the process is right, results are bound to come.

But what's this concept of balanced goals?

Let me explain this to you in simple words.

Virat is obsessed with being fit, and with taking singles and doubles.

I am obsessed with staying cool and working in the present moment.

Both of the activities don't guarantee rewards, but without these, rewards are not guaranteed either!

In simple words, goals that are related to processes—like getting up on time, sleeping on time, ensuring proper rest for the body, taking a break each week (which Virat started taking, apparently)—are equally as important as breaking records and scoring hundreds every alternate match.

Let's get into some details here. This topic is little deep, but totally worth your time. Understanding the concept of different kinds of goals will not only make you better at goal setting, but also ensure scaling of your business and career to the next level!

Two Different Types of Goals

I believe there are two ways of achieving goals:

A. Goals which are driven by processes—our daily actions, our disciplines, our routines, etc., can be summed up as 'Process-Oriented Goals' (POGs).
B. Goals which are driven by numbers—called 'Result-Oriented Goals' (ROGs).

Both are equally important.

Let's pause and see if you understand what all this means. Because in most people that I come across, this is the area of their greatest shortcomings. It pains me immensely when youngsters filled with passion work hard each and every day, and still reach nowhere. When I inquire into what exactly they are doing, I can see that they are failing either in their process orientation or in their result orientation.

Let's understand POGs and ROGs better with some examples.

Take Adhiraj, for instance. Adi wants to do better at his Class 10 grades in mathematics. He works really hard before the examinations. His only understanding is that solving a great paper will give him the necessary grades. So, he works tirelessly on various question papers in the last week before exams, and tries to get a perfect score. To his bewilderment, he ends up scoring 65 on 100 instead; he is now desperate because he cannot enroll in the subjects he wants to, in Class 11.

Here, Adi just tried to prepare for the result. He just focused on the final outcome.

What he should have done, instead, was to include process-oriented goals such as:

1. Solving difficult problems daily
2. Improving his speed of problem-solving
3. Observing questions that are often repeated
4. Identifying and working on his strengths and weaknesses
5. Learning time-management while answering papers

Let's look at a few other examples of goals where people just focus on results (ROGs):

- Playing cricket for the Indian team
- Becoming the most successful businessperson
- Losing 10 kg of weight in the next 6 months
- Getting a funding of ten million dollars

- Writing and publishing a bestselling book
- Getting selected in the UPSC examinations
- Cracking the IIT-JEE

These results (ROGs) are nearly impossible to achieve if you don't have the process (POGs) in place. Please keep the following in mind:

> ***A process-oriented goal means you work today;***
> ***A Result-Oriented Goal means you work on the D-Day (Match Day)***

In 2019, in an article in *India Today,* after India became no.1 in Test ranking, Virat was quoted as saying, "We obviously have the desire to win big tournaments and we want to give our best effort possible. But if you focus on things which are only based on success then you cannot enjoy the process, and we as a team, we play so well because we enjoy the process."

This statement is powerful when you let it sink in and get to the crux of it.

Virat clearly emphasizes that without the right process, winning big tournaments is impossible.

Similarly, in your office, if there isn't a proper system for communicating with your colleagues, you simply cannot grow.

In a business organization, if you don't foster a level of trust and don't enjoy the process of growing alongside your employees, no matter what you do, you will never achieve scalability.

On a personal level, if you cannot carve out time for your partner, there's no way the relationship will grow or sustain itself in the long term.

The biggest point Virat mentions is to *love the process*. Unfortunately, people love results and forget the process.

> "I don't need to prove anything to anyone. I am following a process and runs will come."
>
> — Virat Kohli, *Sportstar*, January 2022

But the result says—love the process and you will get the results!

So, here you go. Read the following statements carefully and think about them:

1. Writing everyday on LinkedIn is just as important as trying to write a bestseller.
2. Trying to change your eating habits is as important as aiming to go to the gym and breaking a sweat.
3. Improving your running is as crucial as trying to hit centuries.
4. Your desire to improve your English vocabulary

is as significant as creating a viral video on public speaking.

The point is—when you set a goal, divide and *balance* it among the following two kinds of goals.

A. Process-Oriented Goals (POGs)

Studying for exams every day is a process-oriented target.

But just imagine someone studying daily and not appearing for the exam. How will they qualify for the next battle?

I see many people just prepare without a dedicated target... and then they wonder why nothing has happened in their lives.

Just as the process is important, so is the result.

Keep the result in mind while planning process-oriented goals.

For me, as a writer, simply putting down a few words does not guarantee success; what will fetch my book that 'bestselling' tag is my writing skill.

What will improve my writing skills?

- Writing one article on LinkedIn daily
- Writing 1,000 words on a new topic every day

- Or, reading a chapter from a new book each day and summarizing it in 250 words

Why?

Because trying and improving your writing skills on the final day is Just. Not. Possible.

People want to become Virat on the final day.

People try to get their promotions at the last minute.

People try to work on their relationships when it's at a breaking point.

These things are Just. Not. Possible.

So, the next time you set a target to win that beauty pageant, find the process goals involved in it—right from maintaining your body to keeping your composure. So, what's the process for this girl? To practice something that can help her maintain her composure in that final moment of the pageant.

Similarly, to make ₹1 crore in a year, you must find the process involved in it.

To make it to Bollywood, signing a movie is a result-oriented goal. Whether the movie will be a hit or not is a result; networking, taking acting lessons, and keeping yourself passionate by acting as often as possible in spite of rejections, is the process.

Let's take an example from the ROGs list shown earlier: *Losing 10 kg of weight in next 6 months.* The following could be some POGs that tie-in with the ROG.

- To wake up at 5:30 a.m. and go for a jog for 45 minutes daily
- To eat an apple along with a bowl of sprouts or salad every day
- To reduce the consumption of junk food from four or five days a week to only once a week
- To drink three liters of water each day
- To exercise for 30 minutes daily, either in the morning or the evening

If you work on these POGs consistently, the ROG of weight reduction is a certainty.

B. Result-Oriented Goals (ROGs)

A friend of mine is a fabulous writer. She writes amazing blogs and has an excellent vocabulary.

She has finished writing a book of around 500 pages. She hunted down two publishers and submitted her book to them. When she didn't get any response from these two companies, she put aside her book publishing dream, forever!

Now, observe that she practiced 'process-oriented goals' but fell short in her 'result-oriented goal'.

She stopped trying because she couldn't handle the rejections.

The feeling of publishers not responding to her was

so unpleasant that the first thought that comes to her mind while writing a book is: *What if the publisher does not revert?*

So, are result-oriented goals all that important? Is it not enough to follow the process thoroughly? Don't results come on their own at the end of the process?

This is interesting to discuss.

As I'd mentioned earlier from the example of one of my clients, studying every day but not appearing for exams will not lead to a successful conclusion in the exam.

Writing a book but not following up on it by putting it in front of a publishing company for its review and feedback makes the process incomplete, without its culmination.

The point is, both kinds of goals are equally important.

When you don't get results, process is important. When a process is set up for acing the examinations, getting results is a given.

In 2022, I became quite obsessed with increasing my social media followers. I was just creating videos and posting them.

Seeing that they were not performing well caused me a lot of pain.

I would watch other creators make their videos and gain a lot of visibility, which left me feeling wretched.

I was only focused on the numbers, unable to understand what was going wrong.

I began to doubt my abilities.

I felt inadequate, unable to cope and compete at this level.

The lack of growth was driving me mad.

It was only when I started rereading my own content from my book on Dhoni that I began to reflect on the process.

I realized that the results were not showing because the process was not aligned.

- My staff was not properly trained
- I was not hiring competent people
- The topics I was selecting were no longer in demand
- I was not adapting to new content trends
- I was only focusing on video quality but failed to learn and update the audio quality
- Fine-tuning and removal of unnecessary parts was missing

But other creators and my competitors were really doing well.

Now, the process was not matching the standard of output I was aiming for.

I was seeking high-level output with low-level input.

I started:

- Correcting the audio of my videos
- Ensuring the scripts were fine-tuned
- Working on my voice modulation
- Conducting research according to audience demand
- Setting up my processes properly

To my surprise, three of my videos surpassed one million views.

I fell in love with the process.

> ***And I realized that if the processes are set up correctly, results cannot fail.***

Some Examples of POGs and ROGs

Let's look at some different contexts and see how POGs and ROGs can be applied here.

Let's first study the two types of goals Virat may set as a cricketer:

POGs	ROGs
Daily training routine	Scoring a century
Focus on fitness	Winning a match
Practice sessions	Achieving a top rank in cricket
Mental preparation	

POGs in Virat's Context: Virat's daily training routine, his focus on fitness, practice sessions, and his mental preparation for each game are all examples of POGs. These are about the journey, the daily grind, and the consistent effort he puts into improving his game, bit by bit.

ROGs in Virat's Context: Virat's goal of scoring a century, winning a match, or achieving a top rank in cricket are examples of ROGs. These are specific, measurable outcomes that are the results of his daily processes.

Similarly, take a look at the two groups of goals from my standpoint as an author.

In My Context:

POGs: Consistent effort and discipline in the craft of writing	**ROGs**: Tangible outcomes of my writing process
Writing daily	Publishing a bestselling book
Researching	Receiving an award
Reading other works	Achieving high sales figures
Continuously honing my writing skills	Having my book be adapted into a movie or series

For a Startup Owner:

POGs	ROGs
Figuring out a correct product-market fit	Making sure numbers are tracked every month
Building a proper team	Keeping up with the expenses
Researching strategies to outdo competition	Staying on track with the output

I believe process + results and their tracking go hand in hand.

Neither can thrive without the other.

The earlier you learn this in your career, the faster you will grow.

In my personal experience, the secret to growth lies in the maturity of understanding both processes and results.

Some people follow the process without considering the output, while others are so obsessed with achieving results that they lack the patience to set up a proper process.

There can also be a third situation: sometimes, we may become overly focused on the process, and at other times, we may focus solely on the results.

In the chart below, I have included examples of both processes and their corresponding results.

I've listed as many professions I could think of.

This is for my readers from various professions. While I may not know much about everyone's field, the basic parameters never change.

Try it out and write back to me on my Instagram or via email to let me know if this has helped you.

Aspect	Process-Oriented Goals (POGs)	Result-Oriented Goals (ROGs)
Focus	The journey, daily tasks, and consistent efforts	The end result, specific achievements, or targets
Example in Cricket (Virat)	Daily training, fitness regime, practicing specific shots	Scoring a century, winning a match, achieving the top rank
Example in Writing (Sfurti)	Daily writing, research, reading	Publishing a book, winning an award, achieving high sales
Example for a Startup Owner	Developing the product, market research, building a team	Launching a successful product, reaching a revenue target, expanding to new markets

Aspect	Process-Oriented Goals (POGs)	Result-Oriented Goals (ROGs)
Example in Medicine (Doctor)	Continuous learning, diagnosing complex cases, daily patient care	Performing successful surgeries, receiving recognition as a top doctor, increasing patient recovery rates
Example in Teaching (Teacher/ Professor)	Creating lesson plans, engaging with students daily, personalizing teaching methods	Achieving high student pass rates, getting positive feedback from students, receiving teaching awards
Example in Sales (Salesperson)	Making daily calls, following up with prospects, attending sales training	Closing a major deal, achieving the quarterly sales target, becoming salesperson of the month
Example for a Designer (Graphic Designer)	Practicing new design tools, improving portfolio, sketching new ideas daily	Completing a big project for a renowned client, winning a design award, securing high-profile design contracts

Aspect	Process-Oriented Goals (POGs)	Result-Oriented Goals (ROGs)
Example for an Athlete (Runner)	Daily runs, strength training, improving form	Winning a race, breaking personal records, qualifying for a major event
Example for a Chef (Culinary Professional)	Experimenting with new recipes, improving techniques, learning about new ingredients	Winning a cooking competition, getting a Michelin star, launching a successful restaurant
Example in Marketing (Marketing Executive)	Creating daily content, studying analytics, experimenting with campaigns	Reaching a campaign target, achieving high engagement, increasing brand awareness
Example in Law (Lawyer)	Researching case laws, drafting documents, networking with clients	Winning a high-profile case, being promoted to partner, achieving successful settlements

The Bottom Line:

- The zen state of mind, where calm and focus are at their peak, helps us perform at our best towards our goals.
- Setting goals and simplifying them by breaking them into smaller tasks helps us be less scared of our work, making targets and success more attainable.
- To achieve goals, focus on the process, not just the results of it. As Virat suggests, *enjoy the process!*
- Know the difference between Process-Oriented Goals (POGs) and Result-Oriented Goals (ROGs)—their contrasting objectives help us *trust the process.*
- It's the *balance* between the two—POGs and ROGs—which holds the pivotal trick to success. If we understand what needs to be kept in focus, when, and where, then the path to our goals is distinctly visible.

CHAPTER 3

VIRAT KOHLI'S FLOW STATE

In the first chapter, we spoke about backing yourself instead of beating yourself when facing defeat, and how consistency might be boring but also the key to achieving your goal.

In the second chapter, we spoke about how important visualization is, and about the two types of goals—process-oriented goals and result-oriented goals.

In this chapter, I am going to take you deeper into the execution of the task; it's probably my favourite part of this book.

How would you feel if your craft could achieve the best result without any effort? Not sure what I mean? Let's look at this in a different way.

How would it feel to be in a spaceship that automatically takes you to your destination?

Isn't this the stuff of science fiction that we dream about living through?

Well, you'll now learn how to do just that... or at least, in a metaphorical sense.

Your destination could be anywhere:

- For a cricketer, that destination would be scoring a century
- For an actor, it would be about delivering a ₹100 crore movie
- For a writer, it's all about writing a bestseller
- For a doctor, the ultimate prize is saving a life

So, where is this spaceship which automatically takes you *anywhere* you want to go, without your even realizing it?

That spaceship is: *the flow state.*

I mean just being in the state of *flow*, and that's all!

Isn't that puzzlingly simple? Let's look into delivering you this magical spaceship.

What Is a *Flow* State?

A *flow* state of work is the highest form of concentration where control is taken over by your subconscious mind. You must have heard of athletes being '*in the zone*'? That's another term for this mental state of complete absorption.

> *A* flow *state of work is the highest form of concentration where control is taken over by your subconscious mind.*

Here's a small story about Virat's *flow* state.

It was March 18, 2012, and India was playing against Pakistan. If you are an Indian, you know how high the temperature rises when it's an Indo-Pak tournament.

India was chasing a mammoth 330 runs which was far too big a total to chase back then—I am talking about 2012.

Pakistan could secure 330 runs, thanks to the respective hundreds of both its openers, Mohammad Hafeez and Nasir Jamshed.

When India came to bat, it was just the second ball of the innings where we lost Gautam Gambhir on a golden duck.

The 23-year-old Virat came to bat on the third ball of the innings, chasing a massive target of 330 runs. He was batting with his idol, Sachin Tendulkar.

Right from the first delivery he received, Virat looked very composed; as he always says, he has learned to use aggression at the right time.

Virat read the situation calmly, with complete attention. He maintained a steady flow of runs throughout the innings. He knew well that the score was big and what he needed to do was to settle himself in, from the very first ball.

He took Umar Gul straight on to hit right, left and center, keeping the scoreboard moving.

Virat went on to score 183 runs in 148 balls, leading India to a win with 13 balls to spare. He spent 211 minutes at the crease, which was roughly 3.5 hours.

Now, the question I'd like you to ponder here is: *Do you think performing for three and a half hours in front of 121 crore people is just a normal thing?*

Knowing the magnitude of the Indo-Pak game, dealing with the expectations of fans, dealing with his own expectations, handling the performance pressure... all this is no easy task. An average human mind would get distracted, overwhelmed, and may easily lose its cool and therefore, give in to the situation. But this is the case with regular performers, not with peak performers like Virat.

Instead, people like Virat enter their *flow* state, a state where they only see their bat and the ball. They are completely immersed in their subconscious.

> ***Every peak performer learns to get in the zone along the way.***

If you, too, seek to enter that state... then read on, we will learn about it throughout this chapter.

Virat Kohli and Sachin Tendulkar have different personalities. Virat looks aggressive and extroverted, while Sachin looks calm and introverted.

But if you ask either of them how they score so many runs, they both answer, "Shots *apne aap lag jaate hain!*"

> "If I'm in the zone, I'm able to block everything around me, not worry about anything else other than my game."
>
> — Virat Kohli, in an interview with Royal Challengers Web TV, 2013.

What could be his mechanism of action?

How could he achieve the fastest hundred in ODIs, double hundreds in Test cricket, and still continue to break records?

Does it involve practice, or mental strength, or something else?

How *does* he get into that *flow* state?

Is there a meditation ritual? Or, a switch he flips to get into it?

Or...

A routine?

I am sure, if it's Virat, there has to be a routine.

There has to be an element which is difficult for normal people to practice.

Keep reading, what you will learn from here on will definitely make you question the way you do your work...

And the way we look at the output.

Also, the way we execute things.

In corporations, everyone is obsessed with salaries. The package you get comes foremost; rarely does anyone focus on the outcome they give.

Your question must be, how is all this related to *flow*?

I will show you how.

How to Get Into the *Flow* State

Flow is a state which gets the best out of you.

But when?

Only when practiced with absolute detachment from the outcome, and when in search of quality and precision.

I want to take your attention off Virat here. For the next ten minutes, I will explain a story to show you what's the *flow* state and how you get into it.

I read a story on James Clear's blog, and later I sought out the complete version online. It surprised me and sparked an obsession with improving my daily habits—everything changed as a result.

This is the story of a student, Eugen Herrigel, and his teacher, the famous archery master Awa Kenzo, known for his unorthodox teaching methods.

Eugen Herrigel was a German professor in the twentieth century who travelled east to learn Kyudo, the Japanese martial art of archery. There, he began training under Awa Kenzo.

Awa Kenzo's entire teaching philosophy was based on mastering one's mind, spirit, and body in such a balanced way that the target becomes inconsequential.

The process of calming the mind, focusing on breathing, and becoming one with the bow and arrow—reaching a state where nothing else exists—would ultimately lead one to their goal.

Awa Kenzo had Herrigel practice shooting arrows at rolls of hay just seven feet away for months on end. Months turned into four long years.

This monotonous task became incredibly boring for Herrigel, and doing it day in and day out grew extremely frustrating.

He often thought about how he had left his country, traveled so far to master this art, and sought out the best teacher he could find, only to find his teacher's pace painfully slow.

Herrigel began to feel disheartened, reflecting on all the effort he had put in without seeing any progress.

How frustrating would this be for you? Just imagine yourself in Herrigel's shoes: you've hired a trusted fitness trainer, but when you go to the gym, he only lets you walk on the treadmill. This goes on for four long months.

Wouldn't you get tired just thinking about going to the gym?

The same thing happened to Virat, I'll tell you about it soon.

Getting back to the story, annoyed, Herrigel complained to his master and wanted to be allowed to get to the next level.

Awa Kenzo then let him shoot targets kept at a further distance, but Herrigel ended up performing poorly. He wasn't able to hit the target, all his arrows went off course and he started wondering if his aim was poor.

A conversation ensued between master and student wherein Kenzo told Herrigel that his aim wasn't the issue, his approach was.

Herrigel challenged his master that if such was the case, Kenzo should be able to hit targets with a blindfold on. Kenzo told Herrigel to meet him later that night.

When they met, Kenzo silently picked up his bow and arrows, stood in his usual place, positioned himself comfortably and released two arrows in quick succession in complete darkness.

Herrigel knew by the sound of the thuds that the arrows must have definitely hit the target.

He immediately switched on the light and went to check and was astonished when he found one arrow bang in the centre of the bullseye through the target and the second arrow piercing the first through and through.

Kenzo had, in complete darkness, not only hit the target, but the bullseye with both arrows.

Kenzo had mastered his art so perfectly that aiming wasn't any trouble for him at all. His entire being lined up with his focus of the moment. He was in such a state of *dhyaan* that there no chance of any error.

People will tell you that if you focus on your goal, you will eventually achieve it.

But what is the process of focusing on your goal? How to begin? It's not just about thinking 'one day I will be rich' or 'someday I will become very famous'.

There are a few processes to follow in between to actually achieve that goal.

Let's understand *zanshin* further.

Why was Kenzo able to hit the target without even aiming, that, too, in complete darkness?

He concentrated minutely with every part of his being, he focused his breathing, he centered his thoughts, his tools for hitting the target became an extension of his body. He worked every day on his position of standing, bending, holding the arrow, breathing.

He aimed without aiming, giving everything to the task at hand which made him do and redo the task in the same way multiple times. He practiced and practiced his art until it became muscle memory for him.

He was in that state of being super aware of everything that he needed, to be able to hit the target.

And that, my friends, is *zanshin*!

Virat has perfected his game over the years and plays now in the state of **zanshin.**

He can play excellently in any type of situation. His methods are perfectly aligned with one another.

He knows exactly what type of swing which ball would need, where he needs to keep which leg, whether he's across the crease or inside it, how fast he must hit each ball to be able to hit it perfectly, which angle his bat must be at for opening. And a lot more!

He has a perfect understanding of everything that he needs on the pitch to get that century. But he doesn't consciously keep thinking about this. It is now a part of his muscle memory.

This is exactly what is needed for getting into the *flow* state.

When you get into the **flow** *state, you are able to follow the process-oriented goals to achieve your result.*

I'll tell you how.

You've practiced your craft tirelessly, and are now in that zone of automatically doing things because you're so good at it, everything just falls into place for you, and you start having fun with the process.

It won't seem boring to you anymore, in fact you'll start enjoying doing whatever you're doing.

Now, look at what this concept says:

The more you try to hit centuries for the sake of endorsing more brands, the less you are likely to score hundreds.

Why?

Because your mind has been diverted by the prize you will get if you hit that century. If your mind is in any way diverted, you have come away from the steps needed to achieve your goal.

In his interview with Puma (Rising From the Ashes | Let There Be Sport), Virat emphasized, *"Mere liye sab kuch intent hai. Agar aapka intent sahi tha aur aapne puri mehnat kari, you will be fine in anything that you choose to do in life."* (For me, it's the intent that matters the most. If your intentions are right and you've worked really hard for it, you will be fine in anything that you choose to do in life.)

Getting into the *flow* state requires intention.

A strong intent to bring about change.

A strong intent to spark a personal revolution.

A strong intent to take on responsibility.

It is this intent that fuels your journey towards the destination you desire.

As Virat has often said, "My country has put me here not for fun, but to take responsibility and not disappoint 145 crore people."

What is your intent? What is your responsibility?

A Little About *Zanshin*

Zanshin is a word used in Japanese martial arts to refer to a state of relaxed alertness. The purpose of this state of awareness is to ensure that you're always ready to respond to whatever happens around you. But that doesn't mean that you are always tense, anticipating the next attack.

Instead, you need to learn to relax and get your breathing right. Only in this way do your reflexes take over, and you respond appropriately and swiftly, without even thinking about it.

Doesn't that sound like a superhuman power?

The literal translation of *zanshin* is "the mind with no remainder." It describes a state of mind when there is complete focus and awareness of the body.

In his book *Zen in the Art of Archery*, Herrigel describes the details of his story and explains how *zanshin* led to a significant improvement in his archery. Give this book a read or listen to it as an audiobook—I highly recommend it. Herrigel says that in *zanshin* lay the secret to mastering the art of focus and concentration.

The harder you try, the less focused you become.

So the idea is to be detached as well as to be in the zone. The idea is to practice and let your body and senses take over.

During an interview with Abhishek Ganguly, Managing Director, Puma, India & SEA, for the Let There Be Sport Conclave, Virat said, "That lesson for me was stop using this (gestures to his head/brain) so much that it actually pushes you away from the real magic. When you just go for it and decide to just play, that's when the magic happens!"

In fact, the above statement trended on Instagram later.

The more relaxed the state of our mind and body, the more likely we'll stay focused, avoid distractions and achieve our goals in the process.

It's so simple, yet so profound.

By shifting our focus away from the outcome and towards the process, we can significantly improve the odds of achieving success in whatever we do.

The next time you're struggling to stay focused on your work, relationships, health or finances, just remember this:

- Forget the goal
- Aim without aiming
- Be in a state of relaxed alertness

Zanshin is that art, that guidance system of your spaceship, which effortlessly takes you from A to B.

Like I always say, follow the process, and the results will automatically arrive. I have written a complete chapter on this in my book *Think and Win like Dhoni*.

Virat Following the Art of *Zanshin*

Virat wanted to learn powerlifting. But for two whole months, he was just lifting a stick.

It was a very boring task for an international cricketer who was trying to get to the next level. But he had to settle for lifting a stick over and over—which would not produce the kind of strength and muscle he was looking for.

Isn't that crazy?

Lifting just a stick, every single day.

Virat said in an interview to *India Today* in 2019 that he was annoyed after one point and felt like giving up. But his coach said, "Trust me, just give this a go." He assured Virat that even if he didn't see the importance of practicing with a stick, going ahead with it would help him get what he wanted, a hundred percent.

The coach promised that Virat would soon lift huge weights and build the strength which he desired.

And this marked the start of those amazing powerlifts which cannot be ignored.

You can see it on Instagram, Virat doing those big

powerlifts and displaying a fitness level which set a completely new standard for the Indian cricket team.

Here again, *zanshin* played a very important role.

Virat was *doing without doing.*

He was *aiming without aiming.*

He understood his craft so deeply, so intuitively, that mastering it became almost subconscious.

> "I always had a sense of discipline in me. However, there was a time when I couldn't divide my time properly between off-field things and on-field assignments. The focus would be missing at times, and that would affect my preparation for matches. I managed to change that."
>
> — Virat Kohli in an interview with *The Times of India*, 2012.

Take a look at some things Virat achieved as he mastered time management and focus, over the years:

- Kohli is considered the fastest runner in international cricket
- He has rapidly accumulated runs in ODIs as follows:
    - 8,000 runs (175 games)
    - 9,000 runs (194 games)
    - 10,000 runs (205 games)
    - 11,000 runs (222 games)

    » 12,000 runs (242 games)
- Kohli has the most Player-of-the-Series awards in T20s (7 times)

Doesn't it seem that he has built his career over all these years in a state of *flow*?

Experiencing *Flow* in Our Daily Lives

Think about this: Starting a gym routine is easy, but maintaining it for a lifetime is incredibly difficult, isn't it?

What happens to us? Why do we drop it halfway?

Is it because of distractions?

Or, is it because we never really care about the process?

Maybe, we're just focused on results. And if the result isn't immediately visible, we start doubting if it's even meant for us.

> ***Next time you start a new routine, try this: Be in zanshin.***

Forget the goal.

Aim without aiming.

The idea is to focus on your breathing and get into that zone where your subconscious takes over.

Even if it's a repetitive, boring gym routine that seems to be leading nowhere.

Virat talks a lot about *selective focus*. He eats, practices, sleeps, and repeats things, over and over, until he gets it.

To make it very simple for my readers and help them convert their small goals into big ones, half-finished tasks into complete and glorified endings, I am giving you a simple technique below.

Just go through with it.

Task for You

When a cricketer like Virat is preparing for a game, all he has on his mind is the next game... And that's the beauty.

In a six-match ODI tournament, the entire team will go one match at a time. They will never overcomplicate things by putting in too much energy.

When we, ordinary people, have a full platter to eat, instead of going one by one... most of us get stressed about finishing the complete platter in one go.

Remember, one bite at a time is the way to go. Think only about the next bite, your next small task.

Take on that next little task you have to complete, in a state of *flow*.

Being in *Flow* Vs. Not Being in *Flow*

As you gain the experience of being in a state of *flow*, you'll notice how it differs from your normal state. Look at the following table. Especially notice the traits of the *flow* state, so you can look forward to these in your practice.

Table comparing the states of being *In Flow* and *Not In Flow*

In Flow State	Not In Flow State
Deep Focus—Complete immersion in the task with undivided attention	Easily Distracted—Unable to maintain focus, frequently interrupted by external or internal distractions
Time Distortion—Losing track of time because of deep engagement in the activity.	Time Awareness—Constantly checking the clock, feeling like time is dragging.
Effortlessness—Tasks feel smooth and effortless despite challenges.	Struggle—Tasks feel difficult or forced, requiring significant effort
High Productivity—Achieving high levels of productivity and creativity.	Low Productivity—Minimal progress, creativity feels blocked.
Enjoyment—Feeling joy and satisfaction in the process, not just the outcome.	Frustration—Feeling irritated or unhappy with the task, leading to dissatisfaction

To be in a flow state, aiming without aiming is important.

As Virat said earlier, "Shots *apne aap lag jaate hain*!" (The shots just happen.)

That means, somewhere along the way, the body has reached that level of *flow*.

A *flow* state of work can also be applied while solving math problems. Then you won't feel like you're solving a paper, instead, it'll be like a game to you!

But for that, you will have to practice the art of detaching yourself from the target, the result, and the rewards.

Virat didn't become who he is because he wanted to be a brand ambassador of so many brands; he became today's Virat because he wanted to score runs against all the tough teams of the world and make his country proud.

Virat has scored centuries against all teams, whether strong or average. This shows his accuracy in the game.

This means, irrespective of the target (opposite teams), he's mastered his art so well that he can play in any condition.

In an interview with Graham Bensinger of in 2021, Virat admitted, "I've always liked to take control of the situation."

For me, when I am on stage and talking to multiple people, I automatically get into the *flow* state and speak. My task and I become one, everything I want to tell the world just effortlessly flows through me. I forget about time, I forget about my initial hesitancy, I forget about everything. My entire being is absorbed in what I am doing at the time. Why? Because I am absolutely and completely in love with my craft. Time flows by and I don't realize it.

You must have seen a dancer, a painter, a musician, a cook, or anybody with a passion for his or her craft doing their work in the deepest state of mind, and not liking any disturbance in the midst of their work. Have you ever noticed this?

Even now, as I'm writing this chapter and everybody is calling me down to go on tea break, in my head I'm like, "*Yaar, disturb mat karo*, I'm busy."

> ***In order to let your subconscious mind take over, there has to be that undisputed belief that you're gonna make it happen.***

And then, miracles will come about.

The Three Cs of the *Flow* State

In this section, you'll learn about the three "C"s I recommend for you, to be in a state of *flow*.

1. Clarity of Thought

Look at what Virat has said over the years.

> "I always wanted to be one of the top players in the world, for sure."
>
> — Virat Kohli, 2017, in an interview with *The Times of India*, after winning the Polly Umrigar Award.

> "I always wanted to be a player that will be known even when I finished my career as a cricketer. I never wanted to be on the sidelines or be one of the players in the side."
>
> — Virat Kohli, 2015, in an *Espncricinfo* article

He continues in the same *Espncricinfo* article, "I had that vision of achieving that goal and playing the way our former greats like Sachin Tendulkar, Virender Sehwag, Rahul Dravid or VVS Laxman have played over the years. I always used to wonder and ask myself, 'Why can I not do that?' I told myself, 'If players before us can do it, we can achieve the same things.'"

All I mean to say is, can you see the clarity this boy brings to the table?

Once the goal is clear, it's very easy for your subconscious to get you the results. It's like asking your driver to take you to Bombay. But if your goals are not very clear, one day you will ask your mind to take you to Bombay, the next day, to Delhi.

And guess what, you would not have reached anywhere at all in this confusion.

To be in the flow, your subconscious mind needs to operate. And for this, it's important to be absolutely clear about what you want.

Even while pacing his innings, Virat is very clear about when he needs to slow down, and when he needs to hit sixes.

He is one of those rare players who will not throw their wicket after getting settled in.

> ***If you have a goal or any target, let it be absolutely clear.***

I, for instance, was very clear that I wanted to build a marketing company, and create a process that's unbreakable.

Youngsters nowadays change their jobs, careers, and relationships, as if it's a part of their syllabus.

Let's not forget an important fact: Virat has been working on his goals, with deep clarity, for twenty years and not just twenty months.

I rarely see youngsters focusing on a single task for twenty days, forget about twenty years.

So, my friend, get absolutely clear about what you want. Go after it, and believe that you are the one who's going to drive the change.

If you have this clarity and belief, then the *flow* is also there in you.

2. Be Comfortable

Now, if my writing has given you an adrenaline rush and you want to do so much... just take a chill pill, readers.

Listen to what Virat says.

> "Desperation doesn't get you anywhere."
>
> — Virat Kohli, to ESPNcricinfo.

When you're desperately striving for results, you can't fully focus.

As Master Awa Kenzo says, if your mind is trying, then you're not truly focusing. Focus without trying—that's the real *flow*!

It's a subtle distinction, but understanding it is worth millions.

At least then, after two decades, you won't find yourself saying, 'But I worked so hard and got nothing!'

If you can't focus, forget about being in *flow* and letting your subconscious work for you.

Virat is known for his intense focus and presence on the field. Whether he's batting, fielding, or leading his team, he is completely absorbed in the moment, embodying the principle of *zanshin* by maintaining a heightened state of awareness. This allows him to react swiftly and appropriately to the ball, the opposition, and the game's dynamics.

When I say 'be comfortable,' it doesn't mean you shouldn't step out of your comfort zone.

That's not what I'm talking about.

I'm talking about being comfortable when you're on the field, when you're taking action.

In a chat with Dinesh Karthik for *Sky Sports* in August 2021, Virat said, "When I step onto the field *I have to believe that I am the best!*"

Virat's basic mantra is: *in any situation, you have to believe that you can get through it.*

Start applying this simple thought in your daily life, and you'll feel the difference.

Message me on Instagram after you've tried it.

You will certainly gain power over the situation.

Even as I'm writing this book, I can feel that something inside me is changing.

3. Concentration

Take the example of the T20 World Cup 2016. India was already down with a bad start, chasing 160 runs

"I always knew that nothing else can distract me from achieving my goal, but the one thing that remained constant was every time I was down, every time I hit rock bottom, somehow I was able to put everything aside and say, 'Right, I'm going to work hard and I'm going to get back up.'"

— Virat Kohli, 2021, in an interview with Graham Bensinger

against Australia. Virat not only took the crease and scored runs, but converted that into a win.

I mean, anyone can start, but only a finisher can take it to the end.

Virat knew exactly when to score a single and when to go for a hit. This level of concentration didn't come from casually learning something on Instagram. Most of us are like Instagram coders or digital marketers who, in one go, want to become the next Virat Kohli!

But his skill was forged through years of hardship. It came from a focused mind that refused to give in to any ordinary distraction.

Flow state is like God's own state, and it comes from extreme hardship, absolute dedication, zero distractions, and, most importantly, believing that you are the best and have the power to make it count.

As Virat says, he keeps moving forward, fully aware that he has to work ten times harder just to maintain momentum.

He also says he cannot take anything for granted. This level of commitment only comes when someone is completely clear about their own expectations and the dedication required to meet them.

> ***Many among us want big things but aren't ready to give what's truly demanded of them.***

This is especially true when it comes to maintaining focus.

Things That Keep Us Away from the *Flow* State

Trait	Explanation
Distractions	Constant interruptions from devices and surroundings that break concentration.
Perfectionism paralysis	Over-analyzing work for perfection, leading to inaction and stalling progress.
Juggling tasks	Attempting to juggle multiple tasks at once, reducing efficiency and focus.
Fuzzy goals	Lack of clear defined objectives, making it difficult to engage deeply in tasks.
The fear factor	Anxiety about potential failure; judgment that hinders starting or continuing tasks.
Energy mismanagement	Poor handling of physical and mental resources, leading to burnout and decreased focus.

Being in the *flow* state is about you losing track of time and flowing with it like a river.

Try being in this state.

And if you are reading this book and lost track of your time, you are already in it.

The Bottom Line:

- To be in *flow*, practice, practice, practice. And then, let your senses take over.
- Don't try to fake things. *flow* cannot be faked.
- Detach yourself from the output, result and rewards. Instead, attach yourself to precision and quality.
- Use the *three Cs* to get into your zone: maintain *clarity* of thought; be *comfortable*; and improve your *concentration*.
- Play with intention, and not just for the output. The perspective suddenly shifts, moving you into *flow*.

CHAPTER 4

TURN EVERY SETBACK INTO A COMEBACK

Let's recap: In Chapter 1, we learned how to keep backing ourselves consistently, despite failures.

Chapter 2 taught us that believing in our vision and following the right processes leads to achieving our goals.

In Chapter 3, we explored how dedication to your craft helps you enter a *flow* state, where your subconscious drives you toward your goal automatically.

Now, you're full of confidence, your vision is sharp, you're following all the processes to the letter, and you're completely in the zone. But you still fail. Now what?

While reading this chapter, take a moment to close the book and reflect on your recent failures.

This chapter focuses on Virat's ability to rise after every bad season.

"I hate losing, and that's the bottomline."

— Virat Kohli, *The Times of India*, January 10, 2015

Just like the setbacks that happen to all of us:

If you're in sales, some months don't go well. If you're a student, you've likely faced rejections in interviews. For a businessperson, sometimes entire decades are spent in losses.

This chapter is dedicated to all the failures you've experienced.

I want you to rise above them.

I want you to believe that if Virat can make a comeback, so can you.

I remember watching a match where Virat was dismissed for a low score in the first innings of a Test against Australia. And yes, there was obvious disappointment in his eyes, but he was unfazed. Remember the backing yourself vs. beating yourself example mentioned in the first chapter?

Kohli backed his skills.

His return in the second innings was magnificent; he scored a century, leading his team to victory.

In another instance, I remember Virat not playing well with the bat, but he still gave an outstanding performance on the field, ensuring his contribution counted.

The Golden Rules for a Comeback

There are times when conditions are in our favour and we end up saying, 'I can do it so well'. But as soon as conditions turn against us, we become negative.

It's on such occasions, however, that champions don't give up; they train their minds to bounce back, no matter what. In fact, their attitudes during crises and adverse situations help us separate superstars from the rest.

What happens as a result of this attitude? You don't lose out on opportunities that come your way.

Once when the Indian team was playing in West Indies, after the fourth ball Virat realized that the pace was too fast. But what he thought was that *he could still play*... unlike the average player who would have thought, *I am afraid, it's too difficult*. And just like that, too many what-ifs and confusion would kill the show.

This incident reminds me of a talk I had given some years ago in one of the best B-schools. I was all pumped up for my talk and went onto the stage full of energy.

I generally start my talks with audience interaction to get into the flow of things. But as soon as I did that with this particular set of students, I realized they were way ahead of me. That brought me down so hard, and I completely ruined the talk.

Had I known what I know now, I would've mentally backed myself on the spot, and carried on the talk with confidence. Virat's attitude taught me that sometimes we can face failure on the field, not just off the field, and we can instantly back ourselves and move ahead.

I do this one thing regularly when I'm at work. I put in my earphones with some calming music which blocks out any noise that may distract me. I then step out of the office and go and sit in the garden.

It's sort of like a meditation ritual for me. I sit there in the sunlight and I reflect on different things in my life. What I like to think about a lot is: how I respond to difficult situations. I reflect upon how I would have reacted ten years back and how I would now.

I have realized that just like Virat, I too, have learned to back myself. Years before, I would have given in to my instant reactions and let the self-doubt and fear win. Today, I can't even remember those self-doubts I had before writing my first book, before speaking on a stage in front of thousands of people.

I have learned that I am my best motivator, I have learned to believe in myself, believe in my abilities, and I know that I can face any challenge head on.

I have learned that I am my best motivator.

Nowadays, when I face a tough situation, I tell myself that if I let go of this opportunity today because of my fear, then tomorrow the fear will return for something bigger. If I can reach for the heights nearest to me, then any new step is as easy as making a jump. It would just need a greater push next time.

A few years ago, when I was writing my previous book, I hit a very tough writing block. The deadline to submit it was fast approaching. The thoughts that continuously kept churning in my head were "*khatam karna hai yaar!*" (I must finish it!) and "OMG, it's not happening!"

This went on for a few days and I did next to nothing in those few days. Then I did my sunlight meditation ritual out in the garden and started processing my thoughts. I realized I had forgotten to back myself.

I immediately started reminding myself of how Virat would react to his blocks, to his hurdles. I remembered how Virat developed this new ability to face a 153 miles per hour delivery, a speed so incredible it's close to being impossible. This gave me such a boost.

I instantly found the inspiration I had been looking for, and rushed back to my cabin. I sat in front of my laptop, took a deep breath and started writing. Words just began to pour out.

Many of you ask me, *how do I come back and retain the same energy after a big potential loss?*

Let me tell you the biggest secret of comebacks.

Arey! But, *thoda toh* wait *karo yaar!* (Oh! But, wait a little!) Have you heard people say this to you?

Remember, Virat was not *the* Virat Kohli of today from Day 1. He kept his nose to the grindstone, maintained his energy, believed that things would turn in his favour, that he could defy the odds. And most importantly, he sincerely gave it his all in the process.

Similarly, whenever you are down in life—be it losing a job or failing an exam or for that matter failing at a relationship—there are some steps which, in my observation, Virat takes to make his comeback.

But you know what, these steps are absolutely simple.

And here come the golden rules that I was talking about. Whenever you want to bounce back after a failed season, just try this, no extra thinking needed.

Step 1: Keep the excitement

Step 2: Stop thinking about what others say

Step 3: Take the help of spirituality

Let's look at this in some detail.

Step 1. Keep the excitement

I think many people who face setbacks, for whatever reason, also fail in their own eyes. They hide alone in fear of the future, and forget the zest they carried when they first started to work towards the dreams they envisioned.

When Virat met the Royal Challengers Bangalore women's team and shared his wisdom with the players before their match against UP Warriorz in March 2023 to motivate them, he said, "I have been playing IPL for 15 years and I have not won it yet. But that does not stop me from being excited every year."

Take my case: I tried making a lot of Instagram videos with the intention of becoming viral and famous, but nothing worked for a couple of years. I kept making these videos just for the sake of increasing the count. After some time, with these videos repeatedly not attracting attention, I lost faith in myself. I lost all the excitement I had for creating new videos. I feel many of us can relate to this sentiment.

And here is what Virat suggests in a similar situation: the real secret is to be excited again! This excitement will do all the magic.

When I saw this interview of Virat, I literally told myself to be excited every time I shoot content, rather than thinking about whether it would be viral or not.

You know how it helps me now?

1. It makes me give my best shot
2. I don't bring my past experiences of failure into the present

So whenever panic and fear starts to occupy my mind, I tell myself, "Sfurti with fear has an almost zero chance to even look for success. But Sfurti with excitement has greater ways to find the path of success."

And, of course, a lot of my videos are performing much better now, thanks to the following I've built. Being present in the moment, and believing that each video has the potential to go viral helps. My enthusiasm for making the videos also keeps me more focused.

Many of us lose our excitement when things don't go our way, but you know what? That's the mark of a quitter.

You never know—the next shot could be the viral one. Don't you agree?

> ***You never know—the next shot could be the viral one!***

Every time we see Royal Challengers Bangalore losing, we feel bad. There are enough trolls and memes going viral about RCB and their bad luck with the IPL. But still, it's Virat and his absolute passion every time that wins all hearts. In fact, he has the most runs even in IPL 2024, with 741 runs.

When I was first writing this chapter, I was watching IPL 2024. Virat had just scored 77 runs against Punjab, and RCB won the game. The way he was running and timing things with accuracy was making me learn so much from this champion! If you see his 360-degree movement on ground, right from his stunning catches to those beautiful ball chases, he never looks out of passion.

In a candid chat between Virat and Dinesh Karthik for *Sky Sports* in 2021, Dinesh mentions a time when, after a bad series, he messaged Virat, "Don't worry Virat, a lot of players have gone through this, you'll get over it."

Virat quickly replied, "Just wait and watch in a couple of months' time!"

This was an interview that was shot in between the matches. And then, Virat won us matches in Australia as captain, where the Aussies were terrified of him. You can also watch this beautiful display of his form on a series called 'The Test' on Amazon Prime Video.

The idea behind all the greatest comebacks is to be excited about them. Imagine what could happen if you were ten times better than you were when you failed. Think about the massive transformation you could achieve to get back in the game.

> ***The idea behind all the greatest comebacks is to be excited about them.***

I'm reminded of a meeting with a girl who was on her journey to becoming a Chartered Accountant. She had already appeared twice for the exam, but failed to get good grades at it. She had it in her to be dedicated to her career, but the results were very disheartening.

So, I wanted to pass on this virtue I'd learnt about comebacks to her. I asked her to replace her fear with excitement, and to start dressing and talking like a CA. After a few months, I loved the transition that was happening in her attitude towards her life.

This made me wonder what miracles excitement can bring to a person. This girl, drowning herself in the sadness of failure, actually got excited about the outcome, and cleared her exam too, in the following attempt.

You know, most people lack excitement, and are also afraid to hire someone like a coach, or approach a teacher to help them achieve their goals or target, but that is the main reason that they don't get the results they desire.

I remember a friend losing her enthusiasm after one failed attempt at UPSC. Imagine her keeping the excitement by visualizing the end goal, and then studying. The same goes for people in fading relationships. Instead of them imagining the worst that could happen, what if they started to visualize the best possible outcome. It's also the same for people going to the gym, while lacking any eagerness for it. Without excitement, the efforts and results reduce by almost 50%.

Everyone drops the catch sometimes, but what defines us is not the miss, but the next catch.

Everyone drops the catch sometimes, but what defines us is not the miss, but the next catch. Dive again, and push yourself with the same excitement you started off with.

Be excited for it all. Dare to believe that it *will* happen.

Sometimes it's difficult to believe in these "miracles". Look up *The Secret* by Rhonda Byrne to help you visualize better and keep the excitement. As I had mentioned previously, Virat was also seen reading *The Secret* early in his career.

You can also attempt a very simple exercise.

> ***Think about any one disappointing result you have received. Now visualize just the opposite of it happening.***

Automatically, a smile has spread on your face, hasn't it? It's just like hitting the gym with full music blasting, and getting excited about the results from your exercise! Think about what would happen if you achieved the result you missed earlier.

Virat says that he was once visualizing smashing English bowlers around the corner. He imagined the outcome, and was insanely excited about living it. This excitement made him do his best at practice, and killed the fear in him. And later, he was also able to succeed in achieving what he visualized.

Just imagine how your life could change once you share that brilliant idea you've been afraid to talk about with your boss. You've kept it to yourself out of fear that it might not work out, but for once, try visualizing the positive outcome. Doesn't that make you feel excited and happy? Take that positive energy with you, and go share your thoughts with enthusiasm, bursting from within.

This feeling will make you work even harder. You will start becoming more disciplined, productive and brisk.

Being excited works, so, *ek bar try toh karo!* (Just try it once!)

Step 2. Stop thinking about what others say

I believe this is one of the main reasons why people are unable to make a comeback. We often focus on the negativity around us and get lost in comparisons—like the one our neighbor aunty makes about her daughter being settled in the US.

> "There has to be something for people to talk about... I'm not really bothered... Something that I've done is to work on my confidence a lot."
>
> — Virat Kohli, *The Economic Times*, November1, 2014

Virat stopped worrying about what people said about him. When he was at his peak, everyone liked him, but when he hit rock bottom, they all disappeared. This gave him the perspective that he shouldn't play for others.

> ***There's no need to prove anything to anyone.***

It's something we can all relate to, right? Think about how it plays out in your daily life. When you're doing well, whether in your job or studies, you're surrounded by people. But once you face a setback, it feels like you're suddenly all alone.

I learned this lesson from Virat during the expansion of my business. There was a time in my journey where, like everyone else, I too, faced a period of setbacks. I was unable to get new clients, and the ones I was working with were also leaving me. My family started to tell me to wind up my business. And my relatives, like in every Indian household, were like "*Yeh kya kar rahi hai Sfurti!*" (What is Sfurti up to these days?) They started to mock my determination to scale up my company to new levels.

That day, imitating Virat's words, I made a promise to myself. This was *my* dream, not someone else's. *I* was the one who stayed up nights to fulfill the dreams I saw with my eyes open, not them. That day, I learned to stop thinking about the people around me, about what they would say and how they would judge me. They just loved the gloomy picture they painted of others, but were not ready to support me or to wait for my success.

This is especially true in our Indian context, where success often brings people closer to us, while failure can sometimes push them away. It's like being the star player in a cricket match—everyone cheers for you when you score runs. But when you go through a rough patch, the cheers can quickly turn into deafening silence.

Don't bother about how others look at your life and your work. What matters is the way *you* look at your life, career, wins, losses, struggles, and challenges. If you think you are a winner, you will win, sooner or later. If you think you are a lost cause, you will lose. If you think, even after you lose something, that you are going to win, you *will* win. Your perspective is the only thing that matters most in your life.

Inthe previously mentioned conversation with Dinesh Karthik, Virat reminisced about the 2014 tour and what followed. He said, "It does not matter at all what people have to say... that's just noise... those are letters typed by someone in the comment section... me and Anushka (his wife) both follow the same thing."

Similarly, when you are trying to bounce back, there are going to be people who will either judge you, dislike you, hope that you fail, or else, outright criticize you.

But here is what Virat said in a news article published by *ABP News* in 2017, "Even now there are doubters and haters all around, but one thing is for sure that I have always believed in myself." He was speaking to them after he'd won the Polly Umrigar award for BCCI's International Cricketer of the Year third time in a row.

Let that conviction win and not the doubt.

Here's my straightforward tip for focusing on your work instead of on other people: Remember why you started. If you're working on something, remind yourself of the passion that drove you to it in the first place. Whether it's your job, your studies, or any personal goal, focus on that initial spark.

Remember why you started.

This advice is simple but powerful. It helps you to keep moving forward, no matter who's watching.

Most people don't attempt a comeback because they are thinking about a specific few people who have hurt them the most.

Maybe it is their spouse, or partner, a relative, or even colleagues, or business partners.

But have you ever thought about whether those specific two or three people are the ones who tried to help you come out of a rough patch in your life? If not, is thinking about their judgments worth even a penny of your time?

My life, right from when I was an engineer, was always surrounded by my passion for cricket and writing. But the day I understood this key, "Let people be," my successes turned into something wonderful to experience.

Similarly, a student appearing for his Board exams spends maximum amounts of his time worrying about what his family, friends, and relatives would think of him if he didn't score well. Half the pressure he puts on himself is of this judgment. If he starts to let go of these thoughts, his chances of doing well would increase at a greater rate.

If a girl keeps on thinking that she is bound to get married early buckling under pressure from her relatives, she might not succeed in fulfilling her dreams. She has to let go of what others say, of those who don't really want her to be happy.

If you, like me, are someone with an ambition to be the CEO of a successful startup, but are bothered by what others talk about you, you will never be able to outgrow their expectations. If today you are afraid of what your family would think, remember, they love you, and that's why they care for you. Even if you face a downfall, they won't ever deny you in their lives. But if you worry about what your competitors would think, you are proving them right by letting yourself drown in insecurity and degrading your own results.

Let's do an experiment. Write down the names of three people who make you nervous:

1. ....
2. ....
3. ....

For me, the first names that come to mind are of my relatives and the competitors in my market. Some days, it gets difficult to match the expectations of my relatives, and to surpass the ideas of my competitors. But I now have a solution to the main issue that takes root in my brain. Whenever this nervousness about *what would someone else think?* makes space in my mind, I flip a switch. Now I instead think about whether they are the ones who are working hard on my behalf; if not, then I just move the thought to my brain's junkyard.

Surveys have revealed that most of the time, we are nervous of the people we are closest to. Here, we should remind ourselves that people who are there for us hold us tight even if we are not able to achieve our desired goals. And about others who make us nervous, let's ask ourselves a simple question, *did we start for them?*

This simple activity will offload your burden and give you hope to stage a comeback with excitement.

Step 3. Take the help of spirituality

> "Unexpected things can happen. Unfortunate things can happen. But the reason why I am here is—there is still hope. There is a 1% chance and sometimes that chance is good enough... Are you willing to give absolutely everything that you have in tonight's game to make that 1% into 10% and then grow that 10% into 30%."
>
> — Virat Kohli during a pep talk to RCB Women's Team in March 2023 (from RCB's YouTube channel)

These words from Virat are also visible in his life. For instance, during the 2024 IPL, RCB was at the bottom at one point, and was on the verge of becoming the first team to get eliminated. But Virat looked at that 1% hope and grabbed it to the best of his powers. RCB was able to find its footing and fought its way up to the Eliminator at Ahmedabad—a feat that seemed unlikely at the start of the season.

You know, a lot has been said and written about the power of faith. It's said that if we keep our faith in a higher power that's guiding us in the right direction, then it becomes easy for us to be on the go, despite opposition.

Spirituality is not only about believing in a religion, but also about completely surrendering to a higher power which will not give you what you want, but will give you what you need. I feel it is about knowing that all things happening around us have deep meaning. The intrinsic point here is, what we desire might not happen right now... but there will definitely be a perfect moment for it to blossom.

> ***It's about knowing that our job is to do what is within our control—that is to take action, to learn, and to improvise.***

It's not in our hands whether we get results; sooner or later, if we have faith and conviction in our inner calling, success and wins will be ours for sure.

Virat himself confessed that he was never into worship or prayer, but is now a deeply religious person. His recent visits to temples in the Himalayas and other parts of the country have been covered a lot on social media. He seems to believe in karma, and is seen carrying the idols of gods and goddesses wherever he travels to play.

Both Virat and his wife, Anushka Sharma, a top Indian Hindi film actress, are known as spiritual people who are at peace with life. They have been motivating people around them even more than they used to, earlier. Their aura and shine in their public appearances only seems to increase.

> ***Have faith in faith and in the power of prayers. Spirituality does help one in bouncing back.***

Personally, when I read *Autobiography of a Yogi*—again a book tweeted by Virat—my goal setting process rose to the next level. By reading such spiritual books, I've learned how my mind functions, and have got clarity about my core principles. It gave me the power—mentally, emotionally, and spiritually—to fight the problems that life throws at me.

Just like Virat, I too started to look for that 1% hope in my life, and to combine that chance with the beliefs that I hold. And you know what? It gave a touch of magic to my work. My personal growth took a huge uptrend just by listening to my core self.

For me, making a comeback is not just about backing yourself, working with mentors, and taking the support of your family and friends. It's also about trusting in the force which is above us all, and that's the essence of spirituality.

> ***In crises, when you don't have anything to lean on, surrender to spirituality, and then see the magic happen.***

In the next and final chapter, I am going to speak about change.

We all need to evolve—evolve to chase the good, evolve to get over the bad. After all, change is the only constant in life. We need to adapt and evolve to survive and thrive with change.

Now as we go to the next stage, I will teach you a method that you will fall absolutely fall in love with.

Read on, this will change the way you think.

The Bottom Line:

- There is no path paved only with success. Every crest has a trough, but being unable to rise again from it is no way to live your dreams.
- It's human nature to be nervous when we face a setback in life. This is a precious moment to remind ourselves of the worth and capability we carry.
- Every loss is an occasion to create new versions of ourselves. It brings us novel opportunities and unexpected ways to succeed.
- When facing a setback, visualize how your life would be once you achieve your goal. This vision gives you zest and excitement to achieve the life that could be, if we succeeded in our dreams.

- It's *your* dream that you are working towards. So, rather than thinking of what others may say, especially those who only love you when you achieve great heights, you should focus on how to better your situation, right away.
- Spiritual books are a great help to comprehend our inner souls. Spirituality helps us stay calm in tough times, teaching us about our minds, and giving us the confidence to take the right action even when unsure about results.

CHAPTER 5

CHANGE AND ADAPT LIKE A CHAMPION

Up until now we've discussed how consistency can be very boring, but if you keep backing yourself, you can do it.

We've understood the processes to achieving our goals. Remember POGs and ROGs?

We also talked about visualizing our thoughts into reality.

Then we learned about how we can get into the *flow* state, concentrating our entire selves into achieving our goals.

And lastly we spoke about picking ourselves up in spite of failure and moving forward.

In this chapter we're going to learn the importance of change.

After hearing so much about how Virat thinks and wins, some of you might say, "*Yeh sab to thik hai,* but *I* can't do it!" (All this is alright, but *I* can't do it!)

It often happens to us, right?

> ***We doubt our worth and think that we can't change ourselves very much.***

Most people wish to change their relationships for the better, to change the way they speak, react, and act, to improve their health and fitness, to enhance their financial status, and so much more. But the question here is, *how to actually bring about this change, smoothly?*

Because changing your mind, especially the subconscious, is not easy; it's definitely not everyone's cup of tea.

As Robin Sharma, famous Canadian writer, tweeted on April 8, 2014, "All change is hard at first, messy in the middle, and gorgeous at the end."

In this chapter, I will give you an effective method Virat uses to implement changes in his batting, diet, thinking, attitude, or for that matter, whatever is the need of the hour.

Vikram Rathour, former India batting coach, said this in conversation with *Sportskeeda* in 2020: "He (Virat) is not a one-dimensional player, he can change his game as and when required."

Virat brought about major changes to his entire lifestyle—changing his diet, his sleep cycle, his gym training, and his cricket practice. He started training harder than ever with that one goal in mind that he wants to represent his country. He is continuously evolving even now.

I know, it looks easy to say change is for the better, but the problem is: how to take the first step?

Find Your Big Reason

You know, being in the self-help industry, I have been trying multiple ways to improve myself. And the biggest issue I encounter is how to maintain changes in the long run.

Just like many of you, I have tried to diet many times, but once I see my favourite white sauce spaghetti pasta, I just give up on it. I dream big, my ambitions are always sky high, but sometimes it gets difficult to maintain that energy and will, constantly. A simple routine of walking every morning feels like a task, forget about changing my entire diet plan.

Do you know what happened recently? My friends decided to go for a drive and I went with them. Due to Virat's virtual presence in my life on a daily basis, I tend to follow him and finish my dinner by 7 p.m. (Yes, of course, there are days when that isn't possible, due to other commitments.) Anyway, I'd already eaten.

All my friends wanted to get some coffee and so decided to go to McDonald's. One of my friends said: instead of just buying a coffee, let's get a full meal. Then, as there were fries on our table, of course I ended up devouring them. You know how these situations escalate. The next morning, when I hit the gym extra-hard, I felt so guilty about scarfing down those fries.

It's amazing and even seems incredible that Virat has adapted his batting style, his thinking, the way he handles media, what he eats and how he eats, etc., while for people like us, just one change (such as regulating our diets) seems so very difficult.

Just look at Virat. Even when he's offered a burger, he ends up just having a small bite. And he definitely didn't eat that burger because it was on his table. Rather, his coach suggested that he absolutely needed to eat well, as his body required it after he scored 235 runs on the field.

Do you want to hear the full story here?

In 2016-17, Virat had a great home season, both as captain and batsman. He narrated a story from the series against England to *Hindustan Times* in 2019. Virat had played an outstanding knock of 235 runs in the fourth Test at Mumbai in hot and humid conditions that had left his body drained.

"When I finished on 235... I was cooked, because during the game I don't like to eat heavy, so I was focusing on bananas and water and... *dal chawal* (rice and lentils)... So Basu sir told me, 'Tonight, you can afford to eat anything you like,' but even then I ordered... a chicken burger, I took off the top bun—I couldn't stop myself—I said, okay, one piece of bread is okay, not two," Virat reveals.

The point here is that in my case, I had eaten my fries without my body needing it, while he ate a burger because it was required... and still he hesitated about eating the bread.

Look at that commitment.

Gosh!

Actually, we too attempt what Virat does, somewhat regularly, don't we? Just think about the time when we started working out at the gym. Was it because we wanted it, or our bodies were urging us to do it? And after listening to our bodies beg, weren't we able to continue it for a significant amount of time?

I am sure there are many people with me on this.

> ***We change, even drastically, but for a very brief period of time.***

Some students completely stop using Instagram when they have exams coming up... but it's so addictive that they are not able to continue with that discipline. Just imagine someone who manages to keep themselves away from social media for one year. The time they get for themselves is 365 days x 4 hours = almost 1,500 extra hours. A few students would do it for two days, maybe three, or at most, five days, but then, the self-control is gone.

What I observed is, these students (and the rest of us, too) lack that *big reason*.

For instance, when you think about representing your country at the highest level... oh my goodness, that's a thrill which makes your reasons pretty strong.

Just close this book and think that you are representing your country in your field.

Did you feel that rush?

I am talking about this high, which can change things for you, inside out.

> *To be able to change, one thing you absolutely need is a strong reason.*

Bring change, by working hand in hand with the reason behind.

You know how I brought about change? What was the reason that drove the change in me? The day I started to manifest my company at greater heights, I knew that if I couldn't be persistent at what I wanted to achieve, then there was no way my dream would come true. That thought is what helps me stay consistent, and to produce wonders.

Strong laser-focused reasons.

> "When life knocks you down, try to land on your back. Because if you can look up, you can get up. Let your reason get you back up."
>
> — Les Brown, an American politician and motivational speaker

This quote is so important and close to my heart. The moment I feel like giving up, I remind myself of my strong reasons to back me up.

For instance, just imagine lazy Bunty. He snacks throughout the day and sits in front of his TV till his eyes pop out.

Today, Bunty's marriage has been set for two months from now.

Will he workout or not?

What do you think?

Of course he wants to look good for his Babli... doesn't he?

Why? Because *shadi life me ek bar hoti hai!* (Because you mostly get married only once in life.) Right?

The reason is pretty strong for Bunty to show up at the gym.

Virat has always been an inspiring personality, and people aspire to learn the way he looks forward in his life. When his father passed away, he knew that this was the point where he needed to work hard to catch up and bring a wholeness to his life.

> "I always knew that I wanted to play the game at the highest level. The time I really thought that I am definitely going to make this my career is when my father passed away. That's the time I realized I got to get serious about this… I became single-minded from then on, just focused to play for India and play for a long time... It was a pure motivation and the will to move forward,"
>
> — Virat Kohli, in conversation with Australian batsman Steve Smith for *India Today* in December 2020

So, it's a very simple and yet philosophical theory that '*When your reasons are strong, distractions become a joke.*'

Once a patient is diagnosed with diabetes, you'll rarely see them eating sweets—because they want to live. It's a matter of life and death.

In another case, if a student knows that he is the only bread winner of the house, he would feel the need to crack his entrance exam by hook or by crook to avoid college donations. Hence, he is highly motivated to study well and get a good rank.

Similarly, a parent gets up every day at 5 a.m. to get their son ready for school because they know: *if not them, then who?*

Very clearly, their reasons are very strong.

I was once an engineer, but my love and passion for cricket were always strong. I began making gradual, consistent changes in myself, and it's because of this transformation that I'm here today—writing a book and significantly growing my business's customer base.

So, dear reader,

What's your reason to change?

Is it about doing something for your country, working for the Indian Army, solving a major global problem, or even losing weight for your wedding?

Or is it that you were hurt in your last relationship and now refuse to let anyone take you for granted?

The idea is to have a reason. A significant one.

If there is no reason involved, then you get a spike of motivation for maybe a day, a week or a month, but it won't last long.

And then you'll again complain, "Oh Sfurti, but I lack consistency!"

Now, while Virat was playing for the Under-19, his reasons for playing for India were pretty strong; he even played the hero at crunch time.

India was facing New Zealand in the ICC U-19 World Cup 2008 semi-finals. Virat as captain displayed exceptional skill as well as determination. He took two wickets off the Kiwis for 27 runs. He also provided stability to the batting order, making 43 runs off 53 balls. His play was not about style; it was all about responsibility and leading India to victory. After his innings, even when India lost three wickets for six runs, the Kiwis were unable to defeat the Indian team, for it had stacked most of the required score by then.

Just imagine a fiery teenager displaying such maturity. His big reason of winning for India, for national pride, helped him adapt coolly to high pressure situations.

How to Identify *Your* Reason for Change

Sometimes, when I ask people *why* they want to change, they give me an answer like, "I want to become a tennis player like Sania Mirza!" But is this reason strong enough? Let's validate it.

Are you trying to become like Sania because of the fame she has, or do you have a genuine love for the game?

I met an entrepreneur who wanted to make it big, for the name, fame, and money that would come with it. He just wanted to become the next Elon Musk. And he was only interested in changing his business all the time. I could clearly see that this person doesn't have a strong reason, and so he kept changing businesses—there was no single enterprise that he really had a passion for.

In the 2016 IPL T20 post-match presentation (RCB vs KXIP), Ramiz Raja asked Virat, "Coaches tell a player to switch on and switch off. When we look at you in the field, when you're batting out there, it's always a 100% switch on. Is that the way you want to play the game?"

You know what Kohli said? "It's three hours of the day, you still got, what, 21 hours to spare, you know, all by yourself to switch off and relax, so why relax on the field..."

When you have a strong reason to perform, changing or adapting is not a problem.

You know there is no reason called a big or a small one; what really matters is how insane you are to grab that reason to change your life. It might be anything, but it has to be what *your* heart desires. And the day you define your reasons, change will complement your life easily and gradually, with consistency at its peak.

But when they don't have a reason, then I see people doing barely anything in life. They find it super difficult to get up in the morning and go to the gym. They cannot improve their language, get better at work, show innovation, or anything at all that'll help them grow in their careers.

So, let's identify what you want to change: do you want to crack the IIM, write a book, look good, or drink three liters of water daily?

Take a minute and ask yourself: **What do I want to change?**

The main point is, whatever the change, *do you have a reason motivating the change?*

Let's do an experiment. First, write down three reasons for why you want the change. The stronger the reasons, the better the results.

1. ....
....
2. ....
....
3. ....
....

And second, is this really what you want, or is it inspired by someone's money, fame, car, or bungalow?

And if it is not inspired by the above superficial factors, trust me, no one can stop you from getting that change you desire.

I'm reminded of a girl, crazy about creating a life filled with success. The major reason she chases change is that she wants to be completely independent in her life, and prove to her relatives—who mocked her very existence and her ambition—that she can do much better than just being a *bade ghar ki bahu, beti* (daughter and daughter-in-law of a wealthy family). This zest she has is the major drive behind her change for the better.

See, she was not going after things that someone else owns. She gave herself a reason strong enough that made it her vision.

Why Strong Reason Needs Strong Vision

There was an interview of Virat's with Puma (Rising From the Ashes | Let There Be Sport) where he spoke about how important having a vision is. He went on to talk about how it is difficult to work with people who are not on the same wavelength as you are, who lack your vision.

Virat said, "You cannot make everyone happy all the time, this is the absolute truth, and why that happens is because certain individuals will not buy into the intensity of what you're saying."

Virat believes very strongly in following the plan. There are many things you might face when working with others: someone might be working at their own speed, someone might not be performing, and someone just hasn't turned up.

> ***Virat believes very strongly in following the plan.***

The plan is not for you to try and take on everything yourself, the plan is to get everybody on board and achieve the goal.

That's the vision. According to Virat that is what's most important.

I have been working on building my own team to handle my company. After many trials and errors, what I eventually realized was that I needed to show them the vision, and motivate them to mould themselves according to the plan. Only then would I be a successful entrepreneur. I started doing just that.

I started setting time aside to work with every individual in my team. We would sit together, have a conversation, and just brainstorm. This gave them that push to perform better, and we were two steps ahead in achieving the vision.

In an article that appeared in *Hindustan Times* in 2021, KL Rahul said about Virat, "Hundred is the best you possibly can be at, but he (Virat) operates at 200. He has the unbelievable ability to carry the other 10 guys and pull them from 100 to 200."

This is his vision, to be the best at whatever he or his team does.

Being Self-aware Is Vital

As per *ESPNcrickinfo*, 2018 was the era which was considered the toughest one to crack for batting in the past 60 years. Test cricket in 2018 provided fewer draws, fewer centuries, and cheaper wickets.

But do you know what Virat scored in that phase? According to the *OneCricket*, he bagged over 100 runs in four matches, and was named ICC Test Cricketer of the Year 2018, and captain of Test and ODI teams of the year 2018.

Just as I do, you might also wonder many times: *what is that key that helps us find the reason to change?*

Virat has a strong belief with regards to this, and it helped me drive my life in a better and more effective manner.

> *I believe the changes that come from within are the best changes.*

Hence, if you want to bring about change, *self-awareness is the biggest driver of success.*

Whenever I find myself procrastinating or wasting time—you know, generally not taking something seriously—I ask myself a couple of questions. It would be useful if you contemplate these questions too.

Question 1. In ten years, will I regret not giving it my all?

And if the answer is yes, I make a full list in my head of what I would lose if I don't operate with my highest concentration.

And most of the time, the answer is ***yes***! Not taking something seriously makes me feel that it will gradually lead me to a loss of interest in my business. After all, if I don't like it, I won't have a consistently growing business. And this would subsequently make me regret that I didn't perform in my twenties with a bit more determination of heart and mind.

Remember, in my first chapter, I said that consistency is boring, but if you back it with strong reason, then boss, you've killed it. For a person with strong reason, consistency is just a small bridge that takes them from point A to B.

During the interview with Dinesh Kartik, Virat said, "I don't want to ever feel, in my life, that I could have done it but I have not. I never want to go back to the field saying, I could've done it, but I didn't."

Virat's words help me function a whole lot better, and I love it when I am able to pass on such words as an easy way forward in the intricate process of growth.

For instance, I met a boy a few years ago. He was studying to clear the NEET entrance examination. But from his words, I got the feeling that his hard work was purposeless. So I asked him, "What if due to some mishap you are not able to pass this paper?" He casually replied, "Will see again, next year." That's when I repeated Virat's thought, telling him not to make any mistake he'd deeply regret when he looked back at it one day. He shouldn't be thinking later, *if only I'd given it my best then, I could be doing wonders in my life right now.*

Close your eyes and think about the task you've been procrastinating on. Make a list of everything you'd lose by not acting with focus and determination. How would it feel to lose those things forever? Allow yourself to deeply feel these regrets if you want a powerful push to spark change.

Question 2: How would this change impact me emotionally?

Whenever you want to make a change, think about your mom, dad, favourite person, or even your country—anyone or anything that stirs your emotions in a positive way. What would this change mean for them?

Research in psychology shows that when you focus on these positive emotional drivers, people around you may wonder how the transformation happened. It's an incredible secret behind rapid change.

Now, Virat has always said that playing at the highest level for the country requires sacrifices. He says he won't take this honour for granted, since he's obliged to fulfill India's dreams in cricket. Just think how this emotional connect has taken Virat to deliver incredible high levels of performance.

Now, close your eyes and visualize the emotional connection you have to the change you want to make. Who would be happiest and most proud if you did it?

How would it make your life and others' lives better? Immerse yourself in these feelings and refill your motivation meter. Now, open your eyes and use that burst of energy to act, right now. Take the next small step towards making that change.

So, the next time you find yourself wasting your time, ask yourself one or both of these questions.

> ***Recharge your drive and keep moving forward.***

High achievers like Virat are definitely much more disciplined than us. But please keep in mind that the dominating factor is a strong reason to perform. Once you find your big reason, motivation is just a spike in time. It's a simple sugar rush that you get, similar to the quick adrenaline high that you get at parties, say by obtaining an iPhone, watching an exciting OTT series, or through shopping. It doesn't really add meaning to your life.

Remember to keep your driving reasons at the forefront of your mind; adapting to the changes around you will be that much easier to achieve.

The Bottom Line:

- To be able to change, one thing you absolutely need is a strong reason. When people don't have a reason, they do barely anything in life.
- To find *your* reason for a change that you want, do the following:
  - » List three reasons (the stronger, the better) you want the change.
  - » Ask yourself whether *you* really want this change, or whether it is inspired by your envy or admiration of someone else.
- You are unstoppable when you are fervent about making a change.
- Self-awareness is the biggest quotient of success in changing and adapting.
- If you're postponing an essential task, ask yourself the following questions to reignite your purpose:
  1. In ten years, will I regret not doing this task well?
  2. What are the emotional impacts of completing this task well?
- The stronger your emotional connection to a change, the more quickly you'll make it.

SUMMING IT ALL UP

I am ending my journey on this book here, the journey I started way back. It's been a long road to travel, one filled with roadblocks. But now that I'm at the finishing line, it has all been worth it.

There's a reason I like to research and write about high achievers such as Virat Kohli and MS Dhoni. They are very different individuals—one is calm while the other is not so calm; one is aggressive while the other is not. But in their own way, they have identified their own strengths.

Think and Win like Virat is an attempt to decode the mind of the champion, and all I could find was the strong reason, intention, and hunger to be at the right spot.

If that is there, then discipline, consistency, accuracy, and goal setting will just follow.

With this book, I am not creating a template for you to copy Virat. Instead, I want you to get inspired by him, to think about what you truly want in life, and then go out and get it.

Chapter 1 of the book is all about consistency. I feel that Virat's most distinguishing feature is his remarkable consistency. I realize that consistency is not everyone's cup of tea. The reason for this is that although we aim to be consistent in our lives, as soon as we face a setback, we lose our will to continue with our essential routines.

If you really want to achieve great heights and big accomplishments in your life, then learn to be like Virat; study the virtue of how he backs himself up, even if he loses an important match of his career.

Next, in Chapter 2, I speak about goals and the power of processes. It's very comfortable to sit and tell ourselves: *I will become the topper of the class, I will crack the competitive exam*, or, *it's my dream to be a pilot one day*. But these are result-oriented goals, where the focus is on the outcomes rather than the process.

What if we instead start thinking, *how can I crack that exam?* Just as when I started this book, my thought was, *what should I do so that it becomes a book that reaches every person who is in need of these words, thus making it a bestseller?* My main takeaway from this chapter is, "The more important the process, the less result-oriented the goals are."

If the approach is right, outcome will be at our doors to amaze us. But if we only obsess about results, and the processes towards achieving them are wrong, then we do not reach those goals.

Then in Chapter 3, I talk about the power of being in *the flow state*. I am one of those people who, if they begin something, have to finish it right away. If someone disturbs me during that time, then I'm unable to bring the best out in me. I love being alone during my work, away from any kind of distraction. People who say that they like to find a corner, with coffee in hand, while doing their work, will completely understand me on this.

When I was finally able to write this book, I understood what Virat meant by 'being in a *flow* state'. I was inspired to find that I could give my everything to the task when in *flow*. Virat, too, states that he is able to achieve the highest score when he is in his *flow*, and now his mind automatically goes into that state.

Discovering my *flow* state has given me an inducement to explore more of such phases of our minds. In this chapter, I have also emphasized the 3 Cs that Virat mentions are necessary to be in the zone (another name for the *flow* state): *clarity* of thought, being *comfortable*, and having *concentration*.

If you, like me, look forward to being in the zone where you become a peak performer, then I highly recommend that you to go through this chapter once more, and you will find yourself having an immense zest for life.

Chapter 4 of this book is about how to make a comeback after a defeat in life. It makes me wonder how Virat has been doing this for almost 20 years now, even after facing many setbacks in his career. Learning about Virat and his dedication to his craft, I can see that that it's his passion that drives him back to life.

Virat came up with some steps that helped him and also inspired me to reignite my life and bag success the second time around. Virat says that he brings excitement whenever life offers him failures. Even when others talk about him or criticize him, he prefers not to listen to them. And he focuses on the power of spirituality to bring him positive energy. This process and his determination help him come back a better version of himself.

In my final chapter of this book, I wanted to share that it's human to have days when we don't have the strength to get up. Days when we might lose our jobs, parents, partners, best friends, or our money. Those are the days when life is difficult and doesn't seem worth it. But this is the most important time to remind ourselves that we need to just adapt to the situation.

Virat, too, may not have been the fittest and the coolest person before; but he adapted a new diet, changed his batting style, changed his fitness regimen, and did much more to become the person he is today.

He controlled his aggression and changed his outlook because he had a compelling vision for his life. If his vision had not been strong enough, then these changes would not have been possible.

The reason why we are not able to bring about change easily is not that we don't have a motive for change; rather, the motive is not strong enough to help us continue with the change in the long run. When the reasons for the change we desire are superficial, we are easily bored and the superficial vision winds up. So, I believe and strongly recommend that if you have a strong vision for something, then you will definitely be able to change and adapt, permanently.

So, my friend, make it a point that you don't just read this book as a Virat fan. Try and apply what you learn here to observe and change yourself in the aspects you feel you could improve. Learn to make friends with change, and adapt yourself easily to new situations.

Even if you're not consistent, read the first chapter again and become consistent. Back yourself up when things are not going your way, and discover the reason why you're not able to stay consistent. Once you get a taste of outcomes from consistency, you automatically get an adrenaline rush to do something amazing with your beautiful life.

Focus on how Virat sets goals in his life, and discover how to get into the *flow* state where you're never disturbed by anything around you. Be it rain or shine, or people saying things about you, you have the power in you to do it anyhow.

Learn from Virat how to be in the flow state, how to adapt, change, and manage yourself, and the most important part of success—to have a determined vision that makes you do it all.

I hope this book helps you in several ways. If it does, please share it with someone who is looking for such words to come out of a depressed state of life, and has lost hope.

This book is not for those who are casual dreamers; it's for those who are unwilling to stop until they fulfill their dreams. This book is not for people to just post about on social media; it's for people who will just not give up even when they fail.

One story I love about Virat is that when he was asked to undergo an important surgery, he declined it, and instead went through a diet to heal himself. He was so determined about his passion that he would do anything, however crazy it seemed, to keep his dream alive.

Do you look with that spirit and grit towards your life? If yes, then this book is definitely made for you.

But if you have not understood the depth of the message in the first go, please reread the book. And yeah, don't forget to send me a 'hey' on my social media platforms because I believe the world is small, and we may meet each other very soon.

I hope *Think and Win like Virat* was an experience that left you feeling motivated and delighted after reading it. If you did feel that way, do share this book with someone who needs to hear these words.

Happy reading (and rereading) to all of you!

JAICO PUBLISHING HOUSE

Elevate Your Life. Transform Your World.

ESTABLISHED IN 1946, Jaico Publishing House is home to world-transforming authors such as Robin Sharma, Sadhguru, Osho, the Dalai Lama, Deepak Chopra, Eknath Easwaran, Paramhansa Yogananda, Devdutt Pattanaik, Radhakrishnan Pillai, Morgan Housel, Napoleon Hill, John Maxwell, Brian Tracy, and Stephen Hawking.

Our late founder Mr. Jaman Shah first established Jaico as a book distribution company. Sensing that independence was around the corner, he aptly named his company Jaico ('Jai' means victory in Hindi). In order to service the significant demand for affordable books in a developing nation, Mr. Shah initiated Jaico's own publications. Jaico was India's first publisher of paperback books in the English language.

While self-help; religion and philosophy; mind, body and spirit; and business titles form the cornerstone of our non-fiction list, we publish an exciting range of current affairs, history, biography, art and architecture, travel, and popular science books as well. Our renewed focus on popular fiction is evident in our new titles by a host of fresh young talent from India and abroad.

Jaico's translations division publishes select bestselling titles in over 10 regional languages including Gujarati, Hindi, Kannada, Malayalam, Marathi, Tamil, and Telugu. These include titles from renowned national and international authors like Sudha Murthy, Gaur Gopal Das, Swami Mukundananda, Jay Shetty, Simon Sinek, Ankur Warikoo and Jeff Keller.

Visit our Website

Boasting one of India's largest book distribution networks, Jaico has its headquarters in Mumbai, with branches in Ahmedabad, Bangalore, Chennai, Delhi, Hyderabad, and Kolkata. This network ensures that our books reach all parts of the country, both urban and rural.